# Dark Psychology

*How to Avoid Manipulation from People, the Revealed Secrets of Persuasion, Brainwashing, Hypnotism and NPL.*

## By Victor Murphy

# Table of Contents

# Introduction

They say that education is power. Indeed, if learning is power, then knowing about human psychology is what could be compared to having superpowers. Psychology, the comprehension of the human personality and how it works, is a topic fundamental to the presence of humankind. Psychology supports everything from crime to religion, publicizing to financing and love to hate. Somebody who comprehends mental standards holds the way to human impact. Getting psychological education is usually a difficult task. Like the majority of humankind's most exceptional privileged insights, psychological learning is covered profound inside the pages of thick diaries and kept out of the span of the general population. To refine this powerful knowledge into a valuable form would expect somebody to dig through uncountable journals and books, endeavoring to isolate the useful things from the futile.

Dark psychology is a well-known concept in the world right now. You probably won't care for this fact however you can't change it too. So, you have a decision to make: either attempt to stay insensible of something powerful or risk turning into its next unfortunate victim, or assume responsibility for your circumstance and figure out how to secure yourself, and those you adore, from individuals who might demolish you through their savage mental abuse.

People having dark personalities might appear to you like ordinary people, but they aren't as they are sharp-minded, and they know how to manipulate others. They lack empathy, compassion, emotions, or feelings like other ordinary people. They only care about themselves and always try to find ways to earn people sympathy. They portray themselves as innocent, which they are not. Behind your back, they might be laughing

6

at you, but in front of you, they make you believe that they are your friends. Such people are dangerous; they don't care about the suffering of other people. Therefore, psychologists study the behavior of such people to understand them and the reasons why they became like this. Understanding dark psychology isn't only a protective measure. There are thoughts and standards contained inside the universe of dark psychology that can enable you to excel in your own professional and personal life. Nobody is saying that you turn into an insane person; however, you can utilize some of its aspects in your day to day life. This book serves as a perfect guideline as it extensively explains the concept of dark psychology. Every chapter explains a new idea regarding different examples or case studies.

Reading this book thoroughly, you will be able to understand the behavior of people. You might understand what sort people you are living around or working with. As knowledge is power, this book explains the purpose of dark psychology, some facts about it and also the kind of techniques that can influence your mind. It also describes the dark traits, the reasons why people have them, and their effects on general society. In a nutshell, this book is perfect for increasing your learning.

# Chapter 1

## *What is Dark Psychology and how it is used?*

Dark Psychology is the study of human manipulative and mind-controlling behavior to persuade others. Dark Psychology encompasses the human nature that controls the minds of people and manipulates other humans. The idea has been captivating the attention of people for many decades. In everyday life, you may come across many stories over social media or within plays about people hypnotizing or manipulating others to work according to them. Many people in everyday life use the phenomenon to persuade you without even knowing. On the other hand, you also use Dark Psychology for our good.

Dark Psychology tries to understand the perceptions and feelings of people associated with these behaviors. People have fascination as well as fear associated with the phenomenon. Higher authorities or those who are at more top ranks such as government officials use their power to control over the minds of those at a lower status. The phenomenon is well depicted in movies and advertisements. Many ad companies use the concept of Dark Psychology to persuade viewers to buy the products. When it comes to home, you can see the manipulation and persuasion tactics used by parents and kids as well to influence each other to get what they want from each other. Within educational setups, teachers use the concept to persuade students in achieving the desired goals. On the other hand, students also use these tactics to influence teachers to get good grades in their academic performance.

According to Dark Psychology, the hypnotizing and mind controlling behavior is 99% time purposive and goal-oriented while 1% time it has irrational intents. Tactics of persuasion, manipulation, and motivation come under Dark Psychology and are used in internet ads, sales techniques, and commercials. People from all cultures, religions, and faiths have this phenomenon rooted in them. Dark psychologists claim that people engage in these behaviors due to the needs of sex, power, or money.

### *Different Kinds of Mind Control in Dark Psychology*

Dark Psychology encompasses the mind-controlling behavior which comes with various types. It's been ages since people use the technique of mind control to persuade others. When people get to hear the word "mind control" they get negative and positive thoughts associated with the phenomenon. Many theories explain the way government officials use the mind control tactic to power those belonging to small groups.

9

Many people within forensic settings use the tactic of brainwashing to manipulate the people who commit crimes. There are various types of mind control which are used by the people during various stages of their life for the fulfillment of their needs. Types of mind control are used to overpower the subject to obey the commands given by manipulator. There are different kinds of mind control including:

- Brainwashing
- Manipulation
- Deception
- Persuasion
- Hypnosis

## 1. Brainwashing

The most crucial and widely used type of mind control is brainwashing. It comes with the concept where the manipulator influences the subject to change their beliefs from past to take on the new beliefs about any particular thing. In this concept subject's mind is altered by using various psychological techniques. Brainwashing is often done to change the religious or cultural beliefs of a subject to divert them towards other religion or culture. Many times people are forced to change their ideals when they move into a new country, culture or society. However, brainwashing is not always negative. Sometimes brainwashing is done by the government officials or those in authority to follow the laws and regulations peacefully.

There are many misconceptions people have about the brainwashing. Many people consider it as the process of controlling people through while others claim that there is no possible way to brainwash anybody. During brainwashing, various tactics are used in combination to brainwash the person to change his beliefs about a certain point.

Brainwashing involves various approaches and tactics which are applied to the subject to persuade him.

The idea of brainwashing is not new in the society instead there are many examples of brainwashing which you get to know from history. In the past, brainwashing was most widely used on to the criminals. This technique is not just a one-step process instead it requires time and a huge set of steps to brainwashing someone.

## Steps in brainwashing

- First and foremost, step in brainwashing is to keep subject in isolation. Isolation is the key in brainwashing because if the subject will be surrounded by people, brainwashing tactics will not work effectively.

- The second step involves the breakage of the subject's own self. This means the subject is told that the facts, figures, logic, and values he knows are not true. Subject stays at this step for several months to completely believe that they are not obeying appropriate laws, rules or values. At this state, the person involved becomes the victim of feelings of guilt.

- Next step in line is the recognition that new concepts, laws, and values are the appropriate and right one. They are made to choose those new values. Subjects get a full understanding of new ideas and values. They get to know about the benefits of the concepts and how they are better than the previous ones. At this point, they will stick to new beliefs, ideas, and values.

The whole process requires several months or years to complete. It takes frequent meetings and conversation with the subject. Brainwashing is not evil every time. Sometimes friends persuade or brainwash each other for the good.

## 2. Manipulation

Another type of mind control which is widely used is the manipulation of others. The psychological manipulation involves changing the perceptions and thoughts of individuals towards a particular thing. Manipulation could be done with love or aggressively both. People deceive or abuse others to overpower them. Manipulation involves one to persuade others for the good of him no matter how bad it could be for the subject. Some subjects figure out when they get manipulated while others may not be able to do so. Subjects do not figure out that manipulation is done to control their mind instead they just consider it as the way of persuasion.

Manipulation can have done effectively only between the individuals who know each other well. Subjects get to know the true intentions of manipulators when it gets too late. However, if the subject gets to know about the true intentions of the subject before the completion of the process the subject may get to face blackmailing from the manipulator. Manipulator blackmails the subject to reach his final goals. The victim becomes stuck in the situation badly therefore, he needs to obey the manipulator till the goals of the manipulator get completed.

The manipulator does not understand the feelings of the subject and doesn't consider his needs and feelings in the mind. If manipulators need to harm the subject, they will do so no matter what. They don't care about the feelings of the subject no matter what. This is considered as the most dangerous form of the mind-controlling where manipulator got expertise in blackmailing and threatening the subject.

## Traits of manipulative people

Manipulative people get mastery skills in deceiving and controlling others. The worst thing is that it is difficult to understand the true

12

intentions of manipulators as they seem to be respectable and behave nicely. Many times manipulators confuse the person by their actions. They mold the facts according to them and master in lying for their good. Moreover, manipulators often play the role of the victim and act as if you did wrong to them and will make you feel guilty of what you haven't done. For a second, they will be aggressive and next minute they will behave nicely to make you confuse and to target your insecurities. They will be appreciative and criticizing as well to make you keep guessing about their true intentions.

In this section, here are some top traits of the manipulators. This will help you spot the manipulators around you. It is important to spot manipulators for your own safety, survival and to maintain your integrity. Here are the few of the traits/characteristics of the manipulators.

### i.    Manipulators are involved in continuous lies

Manipulators reach to their goals and aims by continuously telling lies to others. They tell what is of their benefit and hides what is not going to benefit their goals.

### ii.    Manipulators involve in guilt-tripping

Manipulators involve in guilt-tripping where they unreasonably blame others. They make people in their immediate relationships feel guilty when they are not available. They will make you feel guilty for something you do not want to do.

### iii.    Manipulators respond vaguely

Manipulators don't make others clear of their questions. If someone asks them any question, they will respond vaguely. They do not make others clear of their concerns and misconceptions. First, they don't respond to people but when they do they answer vaguely.

### iv. Manipulators tell half-truths

Manipulators don't tell truth if they do they tell just half-truth. They manipulate or mold truths according to the situation or according to their benefit. They may hold the main information or if they tell the information they exaggerate it. They tell truth according to their advantage.

### v. Manipulators detect the weaknesses

The most dangerous thing about manipulators is that they detect the weak point of the person they want to persuade. They detect the weaknesses of the person and then use them against the person to make him obey the manipulator. Manipulators blackmail the person for his weaknesses and ask him to follow their directions.

### vi. Manipulators shift the blame on others

Manipulators don't take the blame of their doings. They make others accountable for their words, actions or deeds. They lie on the face of the person and make him accountable for everything they have done. At first, manipulators don't believe that whatever they have done is wrong. They keep them in the fantasy of being right and doing well. They think that they are always right and they are others who are wrong. In case if they admit they have done wrong, they justify it with the excuses to make them clear in front of everyone.

### vii. Manipulators act like a victim

Many time manipulators act as a victim to gain the sympathies of others. Although they do wrong, still they make others accountable for the wrong act and plays the part of the victims. Others consider manipulator as the victim and sympathize him.

### viii. Manipulators easily get jealous

Manipulators can't see others heading forward than them. They easily get jealous of others and try to pull others down. Manipulators get jealous even of their partners or parents.

### ix.    They make others doubtful of their skills and qualities

Manipulators use various tactics to make others doubt of their qualities, skills or even personalities. They make people ambiguous of their own selves. People get doubtful even of the qualities and skills they possess. They start doubting their appearance, and qualifications. Manipulators are frequently involved in judging and devaluing others.

### x.    Manipulative people involve in the silent treatment

Manipulators treat their loved ones silently. They often engage in the silent treatment. Manipulative people bully others silently. Manipulators ignore a person, do not voice his opinions or leave the person completely. Manipulators consider them as if they are powerful and dominant. But in reality, they are high in self-esteem and have a lack of self-confidence. They feel pleasure in hurting others. The silent treatment is the sign of manipulator.

### xi.    Manipulators are self-centered

Manipulators attention is centered towards their own self. They don't think about others instead only think about their interest and likings. The only thing matter for manipulators is their own self and benefits of themselves. Manipulators think of their own benefit and work for it no matter it may be harmful to others.

### xii.    Manipulators involve in indirect Insult

Manipulators involve in catty gossiping where they indirectly insult others. They indirectly engage in insulting others to make them obey manipulators. It is the tactic used by manipulators to influence people.

### xiii. Manipulators offer favors and gifts

At the starting of the relationship, manipulators offer positive reinforcement to the people. They offer gifts and incentives to the people to make a good relationship with them. Manipulators shower expensive gifts and incentives to express the emotion of affection or love.

## Techniques of manipulation

Manipulator tries hard to reach their goal by using various techniques of manipulation. There are various techniques which manipulators use to reach out their desired goals. The most widely used manipulation techniques are as follows:

- Emotional blackmail
- Lying
- Creating an illusion
- Blackmail
- Putting down the subject

### i. Emotional Blackmail

Emotions are the feelings which once a manipulator reaches out can easily persuade the person. Emotional blackmailing involves inculcating the feelings of guilt or sympathy within the person. The manipulator attacks the emotions of the subject and gains the sympathies of the person or makes him guilty for his doings. Sympathy and guilt emotions are enough to persuade a subject and make him obey what manipulator wants. Manipulator takes full advantage and persuades or influence the subject for whatever he wants from the subject.

Emotional blackmailing directly attacks the emotions of the person and manipulator needs to work on the core emotions of the person instead of his physical health.

16

## ii. Blackmail

This technique is similar to the emotional blackmailing but it may or may not involve emotional blackmailing. Blackmailing aims at threatening behavior which could be destructive for the subject. The threats in blackmailing may involve killing someone, snatching the property of subject, or threats of causing any other physical harm.

Sometimes blackmailing and extortion are used as synonyms however, two comes with some differences. These two terms sometimes work in collaboration to give effective results.

Blackmailing takes time to work effectively as manipulator need to know the subject first. The subject gets the information and knowledge about the subject extensively and then attacks the weak points of the subject. The blackmailing could involve the threats for revealing any personal secret of the subject. Then the subject may feel threatening and obeys the manipulator for whatever he wants the subject to do. Within work settings, the boss can threat the employees for firing them from the job or for not giving them promotion if subjects will not follow the manipulator.

## iii. Creating an illusion

Manipulators can create illusions to reach out their final goal. They will work hard to create a picture of the matter in such a way that will influence the subject to obey him. The subject considers the illusion as if it is the reality and makes him obey the manipulator. To prove their point, manipulators also create fake pieces of evidence. Before creating an illusion, manipulator goes through a series of steps. He may first think about the ideas and bring stories which he can use to create the appropriate illusion in front of the subject. After that, the manipulator will take these ideas and place them into the mind of the subject. After that manipulator will step back for a few days and will let subject absorb the ideas completely. After a few days, the manipulator will get back to the subject and make the subject to go with the plan.

### iv.    Putting down the subject

This is the worst technique or tactic one can use to manipulate or overpower others. The manipulator puts down the subject to make him follows his commands. Putting down involves the criticism where manipulator criticizes the subject for his doings. He makes subject down in front of everyone in public. The subject feels down as he does not want to be humiliated in front of the crowd. Therefore, they will go with the needs and demands of the manipulator. Manipulator targets the weak points of the subject and humiliates him for those weak points in front of everyone.

However, when manipulator humiliates the subject, he may not like the manipulator and try to stay away from him. This thing happens because he will get to know that he is being attacked or harmed by the manipulator. In that case, the manipulator will try to build good terms with the subject; this can be done through the usage of humor or sarcastic jokes by the manipulator. Humor is a great way of building up a good relationship with the subject by lowering the barriers between them. The manipulator can even turn the insult of the subject into humor. The victim will not be able to figure out that he is being humiliated. This will help to leave no visible scars on the subject.

Another way manipulators use in putting down the subject is in the form of the third person. In this way, they will not make the victim feel that it is he who is putting the subject down. The subject is considering that as if any third person is putting him down and is talking ill about the victim.

The core idea behind this technique is to make the manipulated person feels that he is far less than the manipulator. The victim gets to a higher status or rank and will make the subject feel that there is something which manipulator wants. The subject then tries to fix the problems and start searching for the solution of problems. He will try to get a better relationship with the manipulator. This will make manipulator overpower the victim which will be the greatest advantage for the manipulator to persuade him.

### v.    Lying

Manipulators always master at lying with others no matter what their intentions are. Manipulators lie most of the time to get what they want or to fulfill their needs. Manipulators lie and hide the truth or facts from the subject.

The purpose of lying is that it may help them reach their goals. Moreover, their whole plan can be accomplished much more effectively than by telling the truth. Telling truth may not help them achieve their goals. A manipulator will tell lies to persuade the subject and to gain his sympathies.

Later on at some stage, the victim gets to know about the facts but it gets too late to fix the things. Even if subject after knowing the facts want to disobey the manipulator, then manipulator may show threatening behavior.

Moreover, while telling the stories, manipulators will omit the part which does not best fit with their needs. He may omit the part or replace it with lies to best fit in with their propaganda. These type of stories makes difficult for the subject to demonstrate whether the story is true or false.

Therefore, it is necessary to be wise to check out who are the manipulators. They frequently use lies to achieve their goals. Therefore, one must not obey the manipulator and be careful of him.

## 3. Deception

Deception can have a negative effect on the subject therefore, it is considered as one of the types of mind controlling. Deception is used for the purpose of changing the beliefs of the subject toward any specific event or thing. Deception may include distracting the subject from facts, propaganda, and masking the true intentions. In this form of mind control, the subject is unaware of being deceived. Deception aims at harming others and manipulator often hides the information from the subject. The information which manipulator hides may protect the subject from any harm. Deception is most common among couples and other relationships which lead to mistrust.

Deception can lead to violation of rules and trust which lead to frustration among couples. Deception is most damaging when occurs among friends or other close relationships as these relationships build on the key of trust. Therefore, partners seek their better half to be truthful to them without betraying them. However, when someone who is very close to them is not truthful to them and is deceiving, they may then get relationship problems with that person.

The core issue involved in deception is in the trust. The subject will never trust his partner again once deceived. However, deception could be positive sometime. One of the partners may deceive others to help him/her out. For example, when someone has said something about the spouse and the other partner doesn't reveal it because the information may hurt their spouse.

## 4. Hypnosis

Hypnosis is also one of the most widely used minds controlling technique. A psychological association defines hypnosis as the cooperative communication within the individuals where one person who is influencer provides the suggestion while the subject responds to that suggestion. Hypnosis seeks many unusual and funny tasks from those who participate in the phenomenon. Hypnosis is widely used in hospitals and within clinical settings by therapists to help subjects deal with various psychological issues including depression, anxiety, pain, and others.

Many cases past have shown that hypnosis helped reduce symptoms of dementia in many clients. The suggestions which hypnotist provide could be harmful or beneficial for the subject depending upon the intentions and purpose of the hypnotist. Many people consider the state of hypnosis as the one who alters the state of mind and which is open to getting suggestions. The person who gets hypnotized often has high attention, fantasies, and suggestion giving behavior.

Many surveys have reported the effects that hypnotism has over the individual. Many people reported hypnosis as a relaxed experience while others associated bad experiences with the phenomenon. Many individuals under hypnotism report it as the experience which is under their conscious control however; on the other hand, many reported it as out of their conscious control. Some subjects can carry out a normal conversation while being under the state of hypnotism.

Ernest Hilgard experiments have concluded that hypnotists use this phenomenon to change the perceptions of thinking of the individual. Hypnosis can be used in different areas. It can treat depression, anxiety, and chronic pains. It has contended to minimize the symptoms of

21

dementia. Hypnotism can also help reduce the pains that a pregnant woman encounter at the time of her delivery. Research studies conducted have revealed that hypnotism has reduced nausea and vomiting within the patients of cancer during or after their chemotherapy.

There are many misconceptions people have about the hypnosis. People consider it as the way of asking a subject to perform the inappropriate acts. Many researchers have argued that hypnosis is very rarely associated with the mind-controlling for negative consequences. However, thinking of the subject may be altered to make him get rid of any bad habits he may have.

Many clinicians and professionals use the phenomenon of hypnotism to help subjects in the improvement of their self. Moreover, clinicians use the phenomenon to reduce the anxiety, depression, and pain of the subject.

## Types of hypnosis

Hypnosis has many types which subject undergoes very often. Different types of hypnosis work differently to achieve different goals. Some types aim at helping the client to cope up with the stress, anger, anxiety, and pain. In this section few of the types of hypnosis are mentioned in detail which will help you to a greater extent:

- **Eriksonian Hypnosis**

The most in-depth type of hypnosis is Eriksonian one because it requires the use of small stories and metaphors. The method is done by someone who got expertise in it. One must have to be highly trained in it to perform it effectively. The method makes the use of small stories to present the ideas which are the requirement of the unconscious mind. This type of hypnosis encompasses two types of metaphors including interpersonal and isomorphic. The formal the command is embedded within the story that is very difficult to understand by the subject. The latter is more common than the later. This type of metaphor is comparatively easy to understand. Such stories come with the moral at the end of the story.

- **Traditional hypnosis**

Traditional hypnosis is the most famous and widely used type of hypnosis. This types of hypnosis involve direct suggestions to the unconscious mind of the subject. This type of hypnosis is best suitable for those subjects who do not ask many questions. Such subjects easily accept the facts and understand the reasons.

Traditional hypnosis does not require you to be highly experienced, trained or professional. The technique works best for those who do not think matter critically or analytically.

- **Embedded technique**

Next is line is embedded technique, during which the subject will get to hear a fascinating story from the manipulator. The story aims at distracting or engaging the conscious mind of the individual. Moreover, the story comes with embedded or hidden suggestions that go into the unconscious mind of the subject. Moreover, the story directs the unconscious mind of the subject by using the instructions. The embedded technique finds the memory of the subject that is needed. The memory shows the most appropriate learning experience of the subject from the past. That learning experience is what helps the subject make changes in his present.

- **Video hypnosis**

The types of hypnosis discussed earlier are the famous one and are widely used. However, video hypnosis is not so popular and is one of the most recently developed types. Earlier forms at helping subjects to face the hurdles which come in their way and make the subjects to lead a better life. However, video hypnosis involves working on existing thought processes instead of hypnotic suggestions. The method is different from the traditional methods of hypnosis.

Video hypnosis is the recent technology but it is the most rapidly growing one. People also started using this type of hypnosis frequently. The reason behind its frequent usage is that 70% of the people consider that it is easier for them to learn things which they can see that the things which they can't see and can hear only.

The conscious level of the subject has visual associations which make the video hypnosis effective. Therefore, it is the choice of everyone. Now a day there are various video hypnosis programs which are available, Neuro-VISION is one of them. This video hypnosis technique aims at altering and training the unconscious mind of the individual by the usage of digital optics. This will help subject get rid of his anxiety, worry, urges and pains. This type of hypnosis is best to make smokers stop their smoking. Video hypnosis can best deal with smokers, you can show them different hypnotizing clips that depict the adverse effects of the. This can enhance the chances of smokers to quit smoking.

Video hypnosis can make an obese to lose weight by showing them the adverse effects of being obese or overweight. Moreover, one can show an obese the benefits of being a smart one.

The subjects going through anxiety and pain can feel relaxed due to video hypnosis. Through video hypnosis, one can show various aspects of a happy life and the consequences of being into depression and anxiety for too long. Moreover, you can compare their life with those who live a happy life, this is a great way of making them relax and get back to normal life.

A spoiled child can get better through video hypnosis. In video hypnosis, hypnotists show the subject with various consequences of being a bad or spoiled up child. You can show them what's future has to offer to such children. Moreover, one can show them the consequences of disobeying parents and getting rude to them. However, if they are not good at school, then one can show them the consequences of uneducated individuals and how their life is messed up. Furthermore, they can be shown the job opportunities they will get in the future with this educational level. These all things in collaboration will make a great difference on the child and he may start showing symptoms of improvements within a few sessions.

Video hypnosis does not take too long to be effective. However, one can start seeing the positive results of the video hypnosis within a few sessions. You don't have to wait for long to see the results. Video hypnosis takes very little to show better results.

Video hypnosis is the best form of hypnosis used by many.

## 5. Persuasion

Persuasion is very much like the manipulation in influencing behaviors of others. Persuasion aims at changing the behavior and enhancing the motivation of the subject. Persuader can do it for the good or bad reasons both. In everyday life, you get to see different examples of people persuading others. Persuasion is important for social survivals as it helps in getting people in one unified form that have different mindsets.

The tactic is most important to use within business settings where one person or party need to persuade others. Ad companies use this tactic to sell out the products they are promoting. Persuasion can be done through words or via nonverbal communication. Words are best for expressing the feelings and information with the word whereas nonverbal communication can help subject understand the reasoning.

Many politicians use this tactic during or before elections to persuade the public through their words. This type of persuasion is not considered as bad because it does not involve harming others. When persuasion is done through logic and reasons, then this kind of persuasion is called as the systematic one. Heuristic persuasion involves persuading behavior due to the appeal to emotions or habits.

Persuasion is the tactic of mind control that is used most frequently. While talking about politics, selling products, convincing parents to get you your favorite product all includes the persuasion. Many people do not know that they are performing this type of persuasion even if when they are using it.

Persuasion is positive unless it comes to target the personal ideals beliefs and values of the subject. Persuading someone to change their beliefs, values or religion have evil intents. People very rarely become the victim of this intention. Persuasion aims at changing the behavior and thinking of the subject.

## Elements of persuasion

There are various elements of persuasion which help in knowing what persuasion exactly is. It is the form of communication which involves convincing others to involve in behaviors they want them to exhibit. The best thing about persuasion is that it allows the subject to make free choices instead of blindly following the persuader.

The sole purpose of the tactic of persuasion is to work to shift the mind of the subject to the desired direction of the persuader. Subjects are open to choose whatever direction they want to go to. If the logic or reasons given by the manipulators are authentic and strong enough to change their minds, then they go with the persuader.

- Persuasion involves various elements which make the understanding of it even easier. These elements are as follows: Persuasive message can be transferred by using many mediums including television, social media, face to face interaction or through radio. the persuasion can be done verbally or non-verbally. The best medium for persuasion is face to face interaction where manipulator can easily communicate his message and can better understand the reaction of the subject. Then according to his reaction, he can further use different logics to persuade the subject.

- Persuasion includes intentional influence on the individual or group of individuals. Manipulator intentionally involves influencing the behavior of the subject. He puts efforts to convince the subject to obey him no matter what. If the victim finds the logic and reasons of the manipulator authentic, he may go with his plan. One thing must be kept in mind that if the persuasion is done without any purpose then it will not be done effectively. Manipulators present with pieces of evidence and logic to the subject to prove their point.

- The best thing about the technique is that it involves self-persuasion. The subject is not forced to go with the decisions of a manipulator. They obey the manipulator if they want to. If they don't consider the plan of the manipulator attractive, he may refuse to go with the persuader. The victim gets the freedom of choice where they can freely choose at which direction they want to proceed.

- Persuasion can be done by using words, sounds or images. Manipulator influences the subject by using any medium. They can use this verbally or non- verbally. They can use words or speech to persuade the subject. Moreover, the manipulator can show relevant pictures to the victim or can even play sounds to persuade the subject. Manipulated people are showed that they need to change their thinking. One can use debate or arguments to validate his points.

## *How to use Dark Psychology?*

Dark Psychology posits that every person has the potential and desire to take control over others and make people operate according to him.
It is applied by using various tactics. Here are some of the tactics many of us use in everyday life to persuade others.

## Semantic manipulation

It refers to the idea of manipulating or redefining the words or phrases which become people assume to have negative meaning or definitions. Governments, agencies, or various branding companies use the tactic to change the perception of people about something negative or positive. The purpose of this tactic is to make people accept something which they would not receive otherwise.

## Love bombing/flooding manipulation

People using love flooding manipulation involve in exaggerated affection, love compliments of buttering. This type of manipulation is often used by those in lower authorities to the higher authorities to make a request. For example, employees use love flooding manipulation to get a leave or increment in payment, or students use it to persuade the teacher to pass them in their finals.

## Reverse Psychology

Reverse Psychology refers to the idea of telling a person to do something by saying the opposite of what you desire them to do. Advertisement companies use this tactic for advertising and increasing the sale of the products.

## Fact flooding

It refers to the idea of explaining the beliefs through facts and figures. Random opinions usually don't work; therefore, using facts would be a great idea. The tactic best works on people with low self-esteem. Salesperson, brand managers, and advertisement companies use this manipulation technique to persuade people in getting their products.

## Choice restriction manipulation

In choice restriction manipulation, a person can give an intended person a specific choice option from where he/she has to make a choice. It prevents the person from distracting and helps the manipulator in shaping the person to choose his wish. Choice restriction manipulation is usually done by parents to make their children choose things according to their choice.

## Withdrawal

Persuasion through withdrawal is often referred to as the "silent treatment." In withdrawal persuasion, manipulator starts to avoid the person.

# Chapter 2

*Purpose of Dark Psychology*

Dark psychology aims at explaining and understanding the behaviors, thoughts, cognitive patterns, and perceptions associated with manipulative behavior.

Dark Psychology provides in-depth studies of the thinking patterns of manipulators to make people understand their motive or purpose behind the manipulative behavior.

Dark Psychology studies the human psyche that makes the person perform hypnotic or manipulative behaviors. Moreover, it helps people differentiate between the manipulator and the person who is showing genuine feelings.

In office settings, Dark Psychology helps the owner to overpower his employees to get optimal productivity. Moreover, owners can make employee-employee and boss-employee interaction effective. The owner via Dark Psychology can persuade his employees to work effectively. The boss can also use positive reinforcement manipulation to influence the workers to work effectively within the organization. On the other hand, employees can use pretending empathy or love bombing/flooding manipulation to persuade their owner for getting increment in payment or to get any other incentive.

In clinics, Dark Psychology helps in assessing diagnosing and for the treatment of clients. It serves as helping the clinician to use Dark Psychology manipulations to get to the root cause of the symptoms. Clinicians can use love bombing, sarcastic jokes, withdrawal of affection, usage of aggression, pretending ignorance, reverse Psychology and many other manipulations to assess, diagnose and treat the clients.

# Chapter 3

## *Manipulations in Dark Psychology*

Manipulation is the crucial point in Dark Psychology, which aims at changing the perception and behavior of the subject. Manipulator uses various tactics to improve the thinking of the subject towards a particular situation, thing, person, or matter. Manipulators use different tactics like persuasion, brainwashing, and blackmailing to influence others to obey them.

It is essential for the layman to know about manipulations which every one of you would have faced in your life. The intention of the manipulator could be to get benefit from the subject or to harm him. the drawback about manipulation is that manipulator does not care about the feelings and needs of the individual. Manipulators don't care about the subjects whether they get harmed physically or emotionally. Manipulators try to control over the mind of others by blackmailing or threatening them or whatever it is necessary to overpower others.

32

Many times subject recognize that they are being manipulated but they do not consider it as the form of tactic used to control or harm them. Some people consider manipulation as a way of leading a successful life. In this regard, manipulators use set of manipulations and tricks to overpower the subject. Few of these techniques/manipulations are as follows:

## 1. Lying

Manipulators are involved in false stories, exaggerations or partial truths. They hide the real side of the story from the subject to make him comply with them. For example, brands usually provide false statements about their product services, which they do not offer in reality.

## 2. Rotating the truth

Manipulators spin the facts to match with their views. This is often done by the politicians who twist the truth to best fit in with their policies and rules. Manipulators in this type of tactic justify their statements by providing fake justifications and clarifications. They spin the statements to match with their ideas or views even when they do not involve any original basis.

## 3. Withdrawal of affection

Manipulators often persuade people by withdrawing friendship and love from the subject. In this way, they mentally torture the subject and make him comply with them. This happens in a romantic relationship when any of the partners do not comply with others. When any of the partners no longer engages in affection, love or compliance, then the other may automatically adapt to the habits and behaviors which manipulator want him to exhibit.

## 4. Sarcastic jokes

The influencer uses sarcastic jokes over his subject in front of others to show the subject of how powerful he is. Negative and mean comments are given to the subject in front of everyone to show the power of manipulator. Many individuals want to avoid these negative and sarcastic comments in front of everyone often engage in the behavior which manipulator wants them to exhibit.

## 5. Make subject feel helpless

Innocent people often are the victim of this type of tactic. Manipulators make the subject feel helpless for his lousy life. At the stage of helplessness, when influencer thinks that he is helpless and there is no one to share his problems or whatsoever. At that point, influencer come as the helper of the individual. Then influencer takes advantage of the helplessness of the subject and makes the victim obey him.

## 6. Use of aggression

To show dominance and power over individuals, manipulator uses aggression. Manipulator uses aggression as a tool to take control of the individual. Manipulator engages in aggression, temper outburst to scare the intended person. In this way, individual get scared, and instead of talking on the original topic, he is more focused on controlling the anger of manipulator.

## 7. Plays the role of victim

The manipulator at this level swaps the part and act as a victim to gain the sympathies of others. He goes to the intended person and gains his sympathies in this way. The individual automatically gets inclined towards the needs and demands of the manipulator and fulfills his desires. This is the most widely used influencing technique by pretenders.

## 8.  Pretending ignorance

In this type of tactic, the influencer does not want to let you know about what they want. The manipulator will pretend ignorance means will pretend that he is ignoring the individual. This is done to divert the attention of the individual toward the manipulator. The individual at some time will comply with the manipulator to make him pay attention.

## 9. Threats

One of the most frequently used influencing tactics is abusing and punishing others. Influencer often involves in aggressive behaviors and threats the individual. Moreover, influencer punishes individual to overpower him and make him obey the influencer. Many times, influencer involves physical violence, mental abuse, and many other punishing behaviors.

## 10. Emotional blackmailing

Emotional blackmailing is another manipulating technique that influencer uses to overpower the individual. The manipulator might trap the individual by emotionally blackmailing them that they don't care about the influencer or are selfish and don't care what's going on in the life of the influencer. The tactic helps influencer trap the individual better and make him anxious and confused.

## 11. Pretending empathy

As you all are well aware that influencers or manipulators don't usually empathize people but if they do so it is for their good. They pretend as if they love or empathize with the individual but in fact, they do not. This helps pretenders incline individual towards him. This is a great tactic to make someone obey you in a very sound and calm manner.

## 12. Positive reinforcement

As you know that gifts and presents are considered as a sign of love and charm for everyone. Gifts enhance and change the thinking pattern of the individual toward the giver. Positive reinforcement is the phenomenon which is used by many people. It involves giving gifts, favorite toys, money and many other favorites of the person. For example, parents give favorite sports car of their child upon graduating with good grades, teachers give the present of gift to their students when they do homework or task efficiently.

## 13. Minimization

This tactic used to minimize the effect of manipulators wrongdoings. Manipulators try to convince the individual that what they did wasn't as harming or bad as it seemed to be. However, when an individual will make the manipulator confront his wrong deeds, the manipulator might consider it as the over exaggeration or overreaction from the individual. In other words, minimization involves minimization of the adverse effects of manipulator's wrongful acts.

# Chapter 4

## *Dark Personality Traits*

Various researchers and psychologists have given different number of dark personality traits. According to Paulhus and his colleagues, there are four different dark personalities that one has to encounter in his everyday life. Those dark personalities are Narcissists, Machiavellians, Nonclinical psychopaths, and Everyday sadists. According to Paulhus, many psychologists confuse the traits of a mysterious personality. Every dark personality trait given by Paulhus and colleagues tends to be outgoing and extrovert, but on the other hand, they have clear cut significant differences.

However, the majority of psychologists have identified the three Dark Personality traits named "Dark Triad." The three traits which come under Dark personality are sociopathy, Narcissism, and Machiavellianism.

People usually consider dark personality traits negative, however not every aspect associated with these traits is negative some come with positive characteristics as well. Therefore, you can say that these traits are both beneficial and harmful. In this section, the three aspects of Dark Triad are given along with an additional trait that is given by Paulhus. To make you clear about these personalities, let's have a look on characteristics of these personalities.

### *Personality Traits in the Dark Psychology*

### 1. Narcissists

Narcissists are the personalities holding the element of grandiosity and are high in attention and admiration seeking behavior. People often get easily annoyed with these types of personalities. Narcissists have a highly elevated sense of self-worth and possess a dramatic personality. There are many superstars in the media industry which possess narcissistic personality.

Narcissists consider themselves as the one who no other being can be. If these symptoms persist for long, it can result in the debris field of suffering.

Narcissists think that they are the most loved entity on the planet earth. They do not get ashamed of their doings and considers others to make apology them even if other people are not wrong. Narcissists don't make an apology; they think others must tolerate and accept them no matter what.

Narcissists do not consider them obeying the rules and regulations set by the authorities. They believe rules are only for others who are below average and not for them because they are above average.

"Everyone has to like and be interested in what you have achieved and what you wanted." On the other hand, narcissists themselves disrespect the achievements of others. They do not show much interest and anxiousness towards other's success as much they want others to show for them. They always remain on the "don't care" mode.

"You must appreciate me and appraise me for my achievements" kind of thinking prevailed in narcissists. They consider others to be normal with them even when they are rude or arrogant. One thing which continuously prevails in narcissists is that they think that others are below them and they are far above than them.

They expect everyone to be loyal and fair to them no matter what they do to others. They hope others to appreciate them or accept them even if they are criticizing them. On the other hand, no one can criticize them specifically in public or else they will be ready to murder you.

"To be in good relationship with me, you must obey me." Narcissists expect others to do good to them and obey every order they make and in return do not expect him to follow them.

Living, working, or spending time with a narcissist can make you psychologically and physically ill.

## Dealing with narcissists

Being surrounded by narcissistic personality, it is essential to know about their traits. Only a person who understands the thinking patterns and the reason behind their thoughts can better live with narcissists. Moreover, you can get your relatives, partner, kids, or other immediate family members get out of this personality type. You can do this, only by understanding and knowing them well. The best thing the relatives, friends, children, colleagues, school-fellows, and coaches can do with a narcissistic personality is to support them.

There are various ways to deal with narcissists and to make the active living possible. You need to start accepting the following things:

•   First and foremost thing you need to accept that you may feel degraded or devalued. Accept that! Because narcissists overvalue themselves and do not keep into consideration the values and self-respect of others; therefore, you may repeatedly feel devalued.

• Narcissists needs, desires must be fulfilled first, no matter what! Narcissists do not see how inconvenient is something to achieve or get. They go out of the way and ask you for the things which may be difficult for you to buy. Try your best to fulfill their needs.

● Always be ready to be treated the way you never imagined. Narcissists treat others very rudely and do not expect others to treat them likewise. In other words, you have to be nice with one who will never behave nicely to you. Narcissists get nice very rarely when they want to get something from you or when they seek something of their own good from you. so be wise while dealing with narcissists.

● Narcissists always think that they are prior than others and have no equals. Therefore, be prepared to accept that narcissists are above than you.

● Narcissists don't have any word "apology" in their dictionary. Don't expect them to apology or excuse for their wrongdoings or mistreatment.

● You may get feelings of shock, insecurity, and inconsistency. Believe that these feelings are real and you have to adapt to these feelings while being with narcissists.

● Narcissists will never obey the laws, rules, and regulations. They don't come up being the follower of ethics code or principles. They only follow them for their own good else these are just the words!

● Sometimes you may be the one to cheer them up even when you are the one who needs to be motivated.

- The only important word in the life of narcissists is "me." They can only think and talk about them. They only talk about their values, codes, and worthwhile ignoring the values of others.
- Narcissists always want to be authoritative and manipulate others. To manipulate people, they often come up with false sayings. When one will catch them lying, they will blame that person for the one who is lying. They don't accept what they do instead impose it on others. Therefore, always be ready to encounter such arguments.
- Narcissists often outburst in anger, therefore you may get the feeling of insecurity. Always be careful as you may get attacked from narcissists.

## 2. Machiavellians

Machiavellian personalities are referred to as the "Master manipulators" and have mastery degree in deceiving others. The victims realize the intentions of Machiavellian very late. The people who are highly focused on their goals, Machiavellians manipulate their thinking and deceive them. In this way, the purposes of the subjects get affected.

Machiavellians don't need any mastery class to manipulate others instead they are predisposed with the qualities of deceiving others. They use others to achieve their goals. People who are at higher levels, status or at the positions of power choose to be the Machiavellians in order to gain power over others.

The term Machiavellians was derived from the name of famous Renaissance philosopher Niccolo Machiavelli. The Machiavelli became famous because of his book, which was of the view that those in higher authorities must be rude and harsh to their employees and subjects. Machiavellians are usually aimed at conquering the world or achieving their goals by deceiving others. The term was named until the 1970s.

During that period, Florence L. Geis and Richard Christie developed the Machiavellianism Scale, and this is from where the name was originated. Different research studies have been conducted to check the gender differences in Machiavellians. It was revealed that the level of Machiavellianism is higher in males than in females. Males are more likely to deceive others to achieve their goals.

The Dark Triad describes three personality types: narcissism, sociopathy, and Machiavellianism. It was revealed that Machiavellians receive less attention than narcissists and psychopaths.

## Characteristics of Machiavellians

- Machiavellians tend to be charming and friendly with others. They use self-disclosure as a tactic to use against others. Machiavellians disclose them to make others share their feelings as well. Machiavellians then use those secrets and feelings of others against them to manipulate them or overpower them. These tricks are used by Machiavellians to hide their true intentions.

- People don't prefer Machiavellians to be in their peer group, at work environment or as the life partner. People might like them to be in their competition but don't want to be any relationship with them.

- Sometimes Machiavellians show as if they are guilty for their doings to get sympathies from others. Be aware of these harming tactics.

- Machiavellians often use threats to persuade others.

## 3. Psychopaths

It is considered as one of the utmost dark traits of personalities and is equally dangerous as well. Various research studies done on psychopaths in prisons and in the community have shown consistent higher crime rate.

It encompasses the personalities which have a lack of empathy for others, involves manipulative behavior, shows antisocial behavior, and involvement in illegal activities (not always). In extreme cases, psychopaths can be your killer, they don't care whether you live or die. Some psychopaths can be murderers, killers, aliens, or violent offenders. It is very difficult to spot the psychopaths as they appear normal and have a very charming personality. It is considered difficult to treat adult psychopaths. Psychopathic personality traits are innate or genetic and a person is predisposed to act like a psychopath. Psychopaths and sociopaths come under the antisocial personality disorder of Diagnostic and Statistical Manual. An antisocial personality disorder is considered to be the root cause of both innate and environmental factors. Research studies have found that men are more victim of this disorder than women. Symptoms are prominent during the early 20s of the person and diminish during his 40s.

There are very little chances for an individual to encounter a psychotic person as according to research studies only 1% of the general population exhibits psychopathic traits. Another research study has shown that about 3% of business leaders come under the umbrella of sociopathy.

At starting when you come across psychopaths it would be very difficult for you to spot, whereas with time the nature and characteristics of them become apparent.

Psychopaths are unable to differentiate between the emotions. They may sometime mistake sexual interest with love or anger with irritability. In short, psychopaths come up with shallow emotions. Psychopaths usually talk more than normal people. They can be humorous or funny and engage in telling others stories. They don't make others feel the real side of them. They appear charming and attractive to others. Many times psychopaths talk about the things as if they are experts but in fact, they know nothing. Psychopaths are highly manipulative and can easily control the brains of others. They are truly the master manipulators. Psychopaths come with elevated self-esteem and sense of self-worth. They have an element of pride and arrogance and always consider themselves right even when they are wrong. They engage in multiple marital relationships and have poor control over behaviors. Psychopaths usually lack long-term goals and deny reality.

## Characteristics of psychopaths

In this section, there are various characteristics of psychopaths mentioned which will help you spot them easily.

- **Charming**

Psychopaths always seem normal and are liked by everyone. When they make small talks they seem like well-behaved and well-mannered. They often draw the attention of people towards them by their personality. They tell people interesting stories and are good at persuading others. Overall they got charming personality and are good at attracting others towards themselves.

- **Lack of empathy**

Psychopaths don't think of others before performing any action. They don't think that their actions can hurt someone's feelings. They blame others for hurting them instead of admitting that they hurt others. Psychopaths lack feelings of empathy, love, and care. They don't forgive people easily. They even get ready to kill someone for their own good and benefit.

- **Aggressive**

Psychopaths have aggressive tendencies and are involved in bullying. Psychopaths bully others wherever they go. First signs appear in their school life. Afterward, they are involved in aggression and bullying to their colleagues, family members, and peers. People who can't fight back or are down to earth are usually the victims of psychopaths. They easily get jealous of others and bully the people whom they get jealous of.

- **Lack of remorse or guilt**

The first and foremost sign that psychopaths usually show is the lack of remorse or guilt. Psychopaths are usually not guilty of their wrongdoings. If they hurt someone, they won't accept it. They may consider the victim as responsible for whatever has done to him. Psychopaths deny taking responsibility for doing wrong to others and get offended when someone tries to make them realize. Instead of accepting their fault, psychopaths blame others.

- **Narcissists**

Psychopaths have a high feeling of self-admiration and love. They don't think of other's good or harm even for a second. They always think that they are superior to others and every other person is inferior. They want others to admire them. Psychopaths consider that others are nothing and what they know is the best.

- **Easily Bored**

Psychopaths continuously seek change and thrill in their life. They get easily bored and want continuous change in their lives. They always search for something novel which can make their lives entertaining and full of fun.

- **Seek power**

Psychopaths always want to overpower people. They want others to work under them and obey them. They think they must be followed by others and others should obey rules and regulations defined by them. In short, they want to become CEO of everything where every other person works under him obeying his directions. They love to be the authoritative figure and control everyone.

- **Risk Takers**

Psychopaths don't think of the safety of them and others as well. They perform the actions whatever comes in their mind without considering that it could be harmful to them or others. Psychopaths engage in illegal activities such as robbery, stealing, killing other people and many other grand crimes. They engage in crimes with efficiency, they don't leave a clue for others to spot them. Psychopaths are intelligent and very well-organized.

- **Deny rules and regulations**

Such people don't obey rules, regulations or laws set by higher authorities. Psychopaths believe that rules or laws are unnecessary and don't have any genuine basis. Therefore, psychopaths are often seen involved in breaking laws, breaking signals, robbery, stealing, and many other illegal activities without feeling guilty. Moreover, they often deceive people in order to satisfy their feeling of envy.

- **Master manipulators**

Psychopaths get mastery in deceiving and manipulating others. They know hundreds of tactics to persuade people and manipulate them easily without making them know their (psychopath's) true intentions. Psychopaths don't show people the true emotions they experience for them instead they fake the emotions. Therefore, the peers and loved ones

47

of psychopaths usually don't understand the true motives of the psychopaths. By using various manipulating tactics, they gain the sympathies of people to meet their needs. They trap people through their manipulating tactics.

- **Involve in continuous lying**

Lying is very easy for psychopaths. They lie even on very little things and matters. Psychopaths are often said to be two-faced. They hide their real self and deceive others by their fake self. The actions of psychopaths don't match their words. Their motive behind lying is to benefit them even if it causes harm to others. Mostly they don't have any good reason to lie but they still lie to satisfy their inner self.

- **Highly arrogant**

High level of pride and arrogance are part of the personalities of psychopaths. They think they are of utmost value and importance and others are nothing. They don't help others even if they can do so easily. Level of grandiosity is higher in psychopaths and they think they must be in power. Psychopaths consider themselves to be capable of doing anything.

## 4. Everyday Sadists

Everyday sadists share many characteristics with types of dark personalities mentioned earlier. But in everyday sadists enjoy the cruelty of others. They feel pleasure to see others in the pain or being the victim of cruelty. According to Paulhus, the people mostly hired in police or armed forces are everyday sadists where they involve in harming behavior under a legal order.

Earlier work done on "Dark Triad" of personality later became "Dark Tetrad" as Buckles and Colleagues Delroy Paulhus of the University of British Colombia and Daniel Jones of the University of Texas El Paso said that sadism is the different aspect of dark personality, therefore, it should be considered as the aspect of dark personality.

## Common actions of Everyday Sadists

Every one of you in your daily life encounters everyday sadists. Many times you are surrounded by everyday sadists without even knowing. Everyday sadists are the one who intentionally or purposefully gives pain to others and feels pleasure in doing so. Everyday sadists can harm others ranging from normal to severe. Following are some of the actions that everyday sadists perform in everyday life:

- Intentionally tries to harm others in order to please them.
- Continuously tries to get someone out of the job.
- Unveil the secrets of the people for which they promised to keep private
- Providing others with financial, physical and mental harm
- Involvement in aggressive behavior. Continuously involves in bullying
- Always try to spoil relationships of people with others
- Aims at spoiling the public reputation of the person
- Seeks to harm the people around like classmates, peers, or family members

Everyday sadists just like psychopaths get charming personality which makes them famous within their social group. They are socially very influential and therefore people cannot identify their true intentions. People easily become the victim of their plans. Everyday sadists think that harming others can be beneficial for them in some way. Many times they involve in harming behaviors just to satisfy their feeling of envious, or they may feel threatened, or for them hurting others may be a pleasurable activity.

### *How to deal with people showing dark personality traits?*

Many of you encounter many people around you who are under the influence of dark personality characteristics. It sometimes becomes very difficult to deal with the people possessing dark personality traits. If you are encountering anyone with dark personality traits at your workplace, your house, peer group, or at your school, you can use the following ways to deal with such people.

## Dealing with narcissists

If you are having someone with narcissistic personality traits at your place, then it could be very unfavorable for you and your company as well. At first, it can disrupt the team morale and harmony. Morale and harmony are the necessities to work within the group or team. Therefore, you need to make narcissists realize how his behavior is influencing the group members.

Within a group, narcissists often want to take credit of the group work. They don't want group members to get the credit of any task or performance. Narcissists have high egos therefore; they want others to challenge them. To deal with such people, come with solid counter-arguments to meet the claims of the narcissists. Moreover, another way to deal with narcissists is to put him in such a situation where he is dependent on coworkers. This will make the person obey other group members and respect them.

## Coping with aggression

The aggressivity of people with dark personality traits could be very dangerous. It is very easy to spot whether the person is in aggression or not. Few symptoms of a person getting aggressive are raised the voice, sweats, face getting red and many others.

When you spot that someone is getting aggressive or you are feeling threatened, then immediately leave that place. Moreover, distance yourself emotionally from that person as well. Furthermore, you can ask various open and close-ended questions from the person.

Active listening is a technique used to deal with people prone to aggression. Active listening is where you listen to each concern of the person and the complete message he wants to communicate. By using these strategies, one can identify the cause of a person being aggressive.

## Dealing with manipulators

Within the work setting, there are large numbers of people who manipulate you. But, how it is possible to differentiate between the manipulators and others. It is very simple! If the person who is praising, you have more Machiavellian tendencies then he will surely be a manipulator.

If you spot someone to be the manipulator, then while working with such people always sign a performance agreement. Later on, if the person

51

denies from the performance or work, then show him the agreement he made.

# Chapter 5

## *Six Tenets to Believe*

It is essential to understand Dark Psychology to view life and people from a whole new point of view. A person must be able to dig out the real purpose behind the actions of people. To do so, it is crucial to develop an understanding of Dark Psychology. Here are the six tenets one must be aware of to gain the knowledge of Dark Psychology fully:

**Tenet 1:**

Dark Psychology is not restricted to one person but is universal. The phenomenon of Dark Psychology is embedded in people for ages. People belonging to all cultures, religions, and societies possess this construct. Wherever you go across the globe, every single person possesses these features with the difference of some to possess low, and others possess high levels. The people whom you will not expect to possess these qualities will come up with the constructs of hypnotism, manipulation, and brainwashing.

**Tenet 2:**

Dark Psychology deals with the study of manipulative human behavior and the thoughts and feelings associated with it. Dark Psychology proposes that the act depicted is rational and goal-directed.

Every person holding these behaviors has a purpose behind it. For example, the manipulative behavior advertising agencies show to sell out the products; children show such action to get their favorite sports car from parents and so forth.

**Tenet 3:**

Due to misconceptions of Dark Psychology as an aberrant psychopath, it was overlooked since its earlier forms. In the past, Dark Psychologists defined it as the active and destructive behavior of the person.

In the present, it is considered as the destructive thoughts, perceptions, and feelings of the manipulator, which he depicts not for a particular reason.

**Tenet 4:**

Dark Psychology does not figure out the severity level of the manipulative behavior but can deem the range of inhumane behavior that is the more or less of inhumane behavior.

**Tenet 5:**

Dark psychology comes with the view that every person has more or less of the potential for violence. According to dark psychologists, the potential of violence is inborn, and further various internal and environmental factors contribute to enhancing the probability of potential.

Most of the time, the behaviors posit a reason to depict, and there are very few incidents when these behaviors occur without any reason. The concept of Dark Psychology is solely associated with human beings who perform the actions without any definite purpose.

## Tenet 6:

To reduce and avoid the dangers associated with manipulative behavior, one must fully understand the underlying cause of Dark Psychology. Knowing the causes and triggers related to Dark Psychology can prevent it from reaching to extreme ends. Moreover, the survival within such people will become easy.

# Chapter 6

*Historical, Biological and Environmental aspects of Dark personalities: how to identify them?*

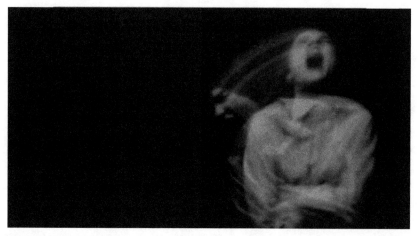

In psychology, the dark personality refers to the character attributes of sociopathy, Machiavellianism, and narcissism, which are designated "dark" as a result of their damaging qualities. Investigation on dark personalities is utilized in psychology research, particularly within law implementation, business management, and clinical psychology. Individuals having high scores on these qualities are bound to carry out violations, cause social misery, and make extreme issues for an association, mainly if they are leaders. Each of the three attributes is adroitly distinct, albeit experimental proof shows them to be corresponding. Each of them is associated with a hard-manipulative relational style.

• Narcissism is portrayed by pretentiousness, pride, self-love, and an absence of empathy.

• Machiavellianism is characterized by controlling and misuse of other people, no morality, and having self-interest.

• Sociopathy is portrayed by constant antisocial conduct, impulsivity, narrow-mindedness, hardness, and cruelty.

At the Glasgow Caledonian University, a factor examination completed found that the enormous five character attributes, the strongest are low agreeableness connection of dark traits, while self-consciousness and an absence of honesty were related with a portion of dark trait individuals.

## *History*

In 1998, Worzel, McHoskey, and Szyarto incited a discussion by guaranteeing that Machiavellianism, narcissism, and sociopathy are pretty much exchangeable in typical examples. McHoskey and Delroy L. Paulhus discussed these points of view at a consequent psychological association meeting, motivating a group of investigation that keeps on developing in the literature being published. Williams and Paulhus discovered enough social, character, and psychological contrasts between the qualities to propose which were different constructs; notwithstanding, they presumed that further examination was expected to explain how and why they overly.

• The idea of unnecessary selfishness has been perceived from the beginning of time. The expression "narcissism" is gotten from the Greek folklore of Narcissus, yet was just authored at the end of the nineteenth century. From that point forward, narcissism has turned into a household word; in analytic writing, given the preoccupation distraction with the subject, the term is utilized more than practically any other. The significance of narcissism has changed after some time. Today narcissism "alludes to enthusiasm for or concern with the self along a wide continuum, from beneficial to neurotic ... counting such ideas as confidence, self-system, and self-esteem, and self-representation.

• Machiavellianism is the political hypothesis of Niccolò Machiavelli, particularly the view that any methods can be utilized if it is important to keep up political power. The word originates from the Italian Renaissance ambassador and essayist Niccolò Machiavelli, born in 1469, who composed Il Principe (The Prince), among different works. "Machiavellianism" anyway could likewise be alluded to the name of a character made by therapist Richard Christie, focused on trickiness, an absence of profound morality, a lack of sympathy, and pessimism.

• Sociopathy, from psych (soul or mind) and pathy (enduring or sickness), was begotten by German therapists in the nineteenth century and initially just implied what might today be called mental order, the investigation of which is as yet known as psychopathology. By the turn of the century 'psychopathic mediocrity' alluded to the kind of mental disorder that may now be named personality disorder, alongside a wide assortment of different conditions now generally classified. Through the mid-twentieth century this and different terms, for example, 'constitutional (characteristic) psychopaths' or 'psychopathic characters,' were utilized all around extensively to cover any individual who damaged legitimate or moral expectations or was viewed as characteristically socially unwanted in some way.

The term sociopath was promoted from 1929/30 by an American therapist, initially proposed as an elective term to demonstrate that the characterizing feature was a pervasive inability to stick to societal standards in a manner that could hurt others. The term sociopathy likewise bit by bit limited to the last sense, in view of translations crafted by a Scottish therapist and particularly agendas advanced by an American specialist and later a Canadian clinician. It became characterized in these quarters as a group of stars of character traits purportedly connected with immorality, or now and again socioeconomic achievements. Official mental analytic manuals embraced a blend of methodologies, eventually going by the term antisocial or dissocial character disorder. Meanwhile, ideas of mental cases/sociopaths had turned out to be famous among the overall population and as characters in fiction.

## Origin

Since the long-debated "nature versus nurture" issue has been connected to the dark triad. Research has started to explore the origins of dark trait characteristics. Likewise, to inquire about on the Big Five character attributes, experimental investigations have been directed to comprehend the contributions of science (nature) and ecological variables (nurture) in the progress of dark triad traits.

## Biological

Every one of dark traits has substantial hereditary segments. It has likewise been discovered that the relationships among the dark characters, and the dark features and the Big Five, are unequivocally determined by individual contrasts in genes. In any case, while sociopathy and narcissism have a generally sizeable heritable part, Machiavellianism likewise is modestly impacted by inheritance, has been observed to be less inherited than the other two characteristics.

## *Environmental*

Contrasted with natural factors, the impact of ecological components appears to be increasingly inconspicuous and represent little—yet still critical—variety in differences of individuals as related to the growth of dark traits. The impact of extraordinary natural variables represents a lot of the difference in each of the three dark characteristics, while just Machiavellianism has been observed to be primarily identified with a shared ecological factor. Even though it requires authentication, a few researchers have translated this recent discovery to imply that Machiavellianism is the utmost likely dark attribute to be impacted by the experience. In any event, this thought about the maintainability of Machiavellianism makes some sense to the extent that the fewer change there is owing to hereditary components, the more difference it needs to be inferable from different variables, and added factors have generally been summarized as ecological in flora.

## *Metamorphosis of dark traits*

A hypothesis may likewise clarify the expansion of dark triad attributes. The contended information is that the transformative conduct predicts the advancement of dark features, yet additionally the development of such characters. To be sure, it was discovered that people showing dark attributes can be exceedingly successful in society. In any case, this achievement is ordinarily short-lived. The principle developmental contention for the dark qualities underscores mating strategies.

The strategy of life history recommends that people vary in creative methodologies; an accentuation on copulating is named a "quick life" methodology, while the focus on parenting is designated a "moderate regenerative" strategy. There is absolute proof that dark characteristics are related with quick life history systems; notwithstanding, there has been a mixture of outcomes, and not each of the three dark attributes has been associated with this strategy. An increasingly detailed approach has endeavored to represent a portion of this mixture of outcomes by breaking down the characteristics at a better degree of accuracy. These investigators found that while a few parts of dark traits are related to a quick life methodology, different segments are associated with moderate reproductive strategies.

## *Components*

There is a decent deal of theoretical and experimental similarity between the dark triad qualities. For instance, analysts have noticed that every one of the three conditions shares attributes; for example, an absence of empathy, interpersonal antagonistic vibes, and relational offensiveness. Likely due to some extent to this correspondence, various procedures have recently been developed that endeavor to measure each of the three characteristics at the same time.

However, a large portion of these methods are surveyed style and want either self-reaction or eyewitness reaction (e.g., appraisals from administrators or associates). These two methods can be tricky when endeavoring to gauge any communally aversive attribute as people who answer themselves might be spurred to deceive. A progressively explicit confound may likewise occur for dark triad traits and Machiavellianism precisely: people who are expert at misdirecting and controlling others ought to be seen low in trickiness and manipulated by other people, and are in this manner prone to get inaccurate ratings. Regardless of these reactions and the recognized harmonies among the dark triad characters, there is proof that the concepts are connected yet particular.

## Narcissism

Narcissists cut a wide and swashbuckling figure through the world. The most benign form might be the alluring pioneer with an overabundance of appeal, whose only bad habit might be an inflated love people. As a distinct difference, there are people with narcissistic character issue, whose vainglory takes off to such heights that they are effectively annoyed when they don't get the consideration of others and profound respect that they think about as their birthright. Genuine narcissists may likewise tend to ignore other individuals' sentiments and exploit others to get what they need. Similarly, as with numerous attributes, narcissism can be seen as a spectrum: Some individuals are lower on the characteristic and others higher, with many arriving in the middle. Outright narcissists display the most elevated amounts of self-flattery. It's effortless to slap the "narcissist" name on somebody who invests a lot of energy discussing his profession or who never appears to question herself, yet pathologically narcissistic characters are moderately uncommon—an expected 1 percent of the populace. Narcissism, as well, is more complicated than it might appear: It's not quite the same as an excess of confidence, including a yearning for appreciation, a feeling of uniqueness, and an absence of compassion, alongside different traits that can harm the relationships. Strikingly, supposing that they are preferable and more deserving over others, researchers recommend, exceptionally narcissistic individuals frequently concede that they are self-centered, as well.

## Signs of narcissism: superiority and entitlement

The universe of the narcissist is about good/bad, unrivaled/inferior, and right/wrong. There is a positive chain of hierarchy, with the narcissist at the top—which is the central spot he has a sense of security. Narcissists must be the best, the most right, and the ablest; do everything in their way; possesses everything, and controls everybody. Strangely enough, narcissists can likewise get that prevalent feeling by being the most terrible; the wrongness; or the sickest, upset, or harmed for a timeframe.

## *The exaggerated requirement for attention and approval*

Narcissists require constant attention. Validation for a narcissist counts only if it originates from others. And still, after all that, it doesn't mean much. A narcissist's requirement for approval resembles a funnel. No matter how much you tell narcissists you adore them, respect them, or support them, they never feel it's sufficient—because they don't accept anybody can love them. Regardless of all their self-absorbed, bragging, narcissists are in reality, extraordinarily insecure and dreadful of not having what it takes.

## *Perfectionism*

Narcissists have a very high requirement for everything to be perfect. They believe they ought to be impeccable, you ought to be accurate, occasions ought to happen precisely as they expect, and life should play out absolutely as they imagine it. This is a painfully incomprehensible interest, which results in the narcissist feeling disappointed and hopeless most of the time.

## *The great need for control*

Since narcissists are persistently baffled with the imperfect way life unfurls, they need to do however much as could be expected to control it and form it just as they would prefer. They need and demand to be in charge, and their feeling of privilege causes it to appear to be consistent to them that they ought to be in charge—of everything. Narcissists dependably have a storyline as the main priority about what each "character" in their interaction ought to be saying and doing.

63

## Shame

Narcissists don't feel much blame since they think they are right in every case, and they don't believe their practices indeed influence any other person. In any case, they harbor a great deal of shame. Covered in a profoundly curbed piece of the narcissist are every one of the uncertainties, fears, and rejected traits that he is continually guarding to escape from everybody, including himself.

## Fear

The narcissist's whole life is persuaded and stimulated by fear. Most narcissists' feelings of dread are profoundly covered and quelled. They're always terrified of being derided, rejected, or wrong. Therefore, they don't trust anyone.

## Lack of empathy

Narcissists cannot sympathize with others. They will, in general, be narrow-minded and self-involved and are typically unfit to comprehend what other individuals are feeling. Narcissists anticipate that others should think and feel equivalent to they do and only sometimes give an idea to how others think. They are likewise once in a while ashamed, apologetic or guilty.

## Machiavellianism

Machiavellianism in psychology alludes to a character attribute which sees an individual so centered on their interests they will control, deceive, and misuse others to accomplish their goals. By the late sixteenth century "Machiavellianism" turned into a famous word to portray the craft of being misleading to get ahead. Machiavellianism has been observed to be increasingly regular in men than ladies. It can, however, happen in anybody – even youngsters.

### Signs of Machiavellianism

Somebody with the characteristic of Machiavellianism will, in general, have a significant number of the accompanying propensities:

- Just centered around their very own aspiration and interests
- Prioritize cash and power over relationships
- Appear to be enchanting and confident
- Misuse and control others to excel
- Lie and deceive when required
- Use flattery words frequently
- Ailing in standards and values
- Low degrees of sympathy
- Often evade commitment and emotional connections
- can be persistent because of calculating nature
- Once in a while uncover their actual aims
- can be great at reading social circumstances and others
- Absence of warmth in social collaborations
- Not always mindful of the results of their activities

### Related psychological conditions with Machiavellianism

Machiavellianism is viewed as a feature of the 'Dark Triad,' which is one of three character traits that likewise incorporates narcissism and sociopathy. With each one of these traits alone making somebody hard to associate with, each of the three happening in one individual can make for somebody that is very hazardous to other individuals' psychological prosperity. Regardless of apparently clear associations between the three 'dark triad' traits and the predominance of one characteristic frequently happening with the other two, research has to be done to prove a correlation. Personality disorders where sufferers may have the quality of Machiavellianism incorporate antisocial character disorder, and

Narcissistic character disorder. Recent research additionally found a high commonness of melancholy in those with the Machiavellian quality.

### How can Machiavellianism be treated?

The issue with malevolent character traits like those found in the dark triad is that the individuals who have such characteristics are probably not going to look for treatment or need to change. They generally possibly go to treatment whenever pushed to do as such by relatives or because they have carried out wrongdoing and have been advised to go to therapy by court request. For psychotherapy to be viable, a patient should be straightforward and enable a confiding relationship to form among themselves and their advisor. Machiavellianism is a quality whereby an individual is frequently untrustworthy and does not confide in others. Cognitive-behavioral therapy is one kind of treatment that is sometimes suggested for those with noxious character traits. It upholds that the manner in which the person thinks directs their conduct, so by recognizing and supplanting disordered thoughts and sentiments he would then be able to change behavior.

### Disorder of sociopathy

The disorder of sociopathy is the most troublesome disorders to recognize. The psychotic person can seem ordinary, even beguiling. Underneath, his absences conscience and sympathy, making him cunning, unstable and regularly unlawful. Psychopaths are matters of famous interest and clinical torture: Adult sociopaths are to a great extent resistant to treatment, however projects are set up to treat hard, and apathetic youth to prevent them from developing into sociopaths. The expressions "psychopath" and "sociopath" are regularly utilized reciprocally, yet in right speech a "sociopath" alludes to an individual with antisocial propensities that are attributed to societal or natural

66

variables, while psychopathic characters are increasingly intrinsic, however a riotous or fierce childhood may be the deciding factor for those officially inclined to carry on psychopathically. The two terms are most firmly represented to in the (DSM) Diagnostic & Statistical Manual of Mental Disorders as Disruptive Character Disorder. The DSM utilizes not one or the other "sociopathy" nor "psychotic," however are these terms generally utilized in medical and common speech. Brain anatomy, inheritance, and an individual's atmosphere may all add to the growth of psychopathic characters.

### *The Symbols of a Psychotic Person*

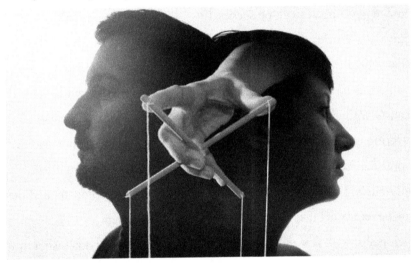

Sociopathy is a disorder that can be analyzed utilizing the 20-thing Hare Psychotic Checklist, which highlights traits, for example, absence of sympathy, sexual indiscrimination, neurotic lying, parasitic way of life, and impulsive behavior. The bar for medical psychopaths is a 30 score or higher but serial killer Ted Bundy had a score of 39. The Canadian specialist Robert Hare created an agenda during the 1970s, teacher at the University of British Columbia named Emeritus. It was initially used to evaluate people in criminal cases or high-security mental units; the agenda things are presently promptly discovered online for anybody to scrutinize. A genuine evaluation ought to be directed by a mentally healthy professional.

### *Psychopaths can never be cured*

In the same way as other character traits, sociopathy is a spectrum. Around 1-2% of men and 0.3-0.7% of ladies in the all general community are assessed to be genuine sociopaths, yet for the remainder of us, you fall on the scale someplace dropdown. Individuals who experience psychopathic traits, for example, savagery, charm, impulsivity, and convincingness, will in general traverse life fine. Indeed, genuine psychopaths can be successful— they just won't ever be equivalent to every other person.

What separates a genuine psychotic person from the remainder of the populace is an absence of sympathy. They will always be unable to identify with another person's sentiments or care that another person is suffering while they flourish. Some of the time, a psychotic person will appreciate feeling unrivaled while they cause mayhem for other individuals. Lacking compassion isn't an issue for a psychopath, and they won't ever accept that there's anything wrong with them.

Sociopaths don't fear punishment or social slander. They don't want to fit into social standards, so desires for society do not affect their conduct. This is the reason if they are sentenced for violations, the punishment appears to not affect them. Reward-based treatment, for example, giving them their preferred sustenance or computer games so that they carry on, is viewed as the best course to oversee psychopaths who are imprisoned. However, even by keeping them quiet, this is a method for control, not a cure.

Not all psychopaths will progress toward becoming illegal, and many will traverse existence without anybody recognizing what they are. In any case, regardless of whether they end up raising trouble or not, there's no proof their character will ever change. Hence, psychopaths can never be cured.

# Chapter 7

## How to use psychology in Daily Routine Life: 10 classic psychological studies on what you think of yourself

Whatever your insight into this science might be, you most likely use psychology in your day to day life, and if you don't, it has presumably been utilized on you, regardless of whether you know it or not.

A few people use Psychology intentionally to help in their regular day to day life. For instance, marketing utilizes psychological strategies to ask potential purchasers to buy the item or service they are selling. That advert that made you cry and constrained you to text '1234' to give £4? It utilized passionate and psychological interests to pull on your heartstrings so you would do what they needed.

Other individuals may utilize Psychology and not know they are doing as such. Listening to a companion's issues and using words like "yes" or sounds like "mm" tells the individual you're looking to them and is a well-utilized strategy in advising. Rehashing words back to the speaker and reflecting their non-verbal communication is another notable procedure to enable the individual to feel calm and agreeable around you. Robert J. Sternberg, Ph.D., is famous for examining to improve the territories he isn't genuinely adept at, including insight tests since he wasn't especially great at IQ tests, love since he had failed relationships and creativity when he became mindful he had more smart thoughts. Utilizing mental research methods, Sternberg created solutions from investigating his exploration, which helped him in every part of his life. Lisa Logan, a self-defense teacher in Cambridge, accepts that through contemplating the psychology of aggressors, she can train her students how to get into the heads of the assailant to beat them. Utilizing psychology to pinpoint how the assailant things can diminish the danger of an assault occurring, and this can be applied to numerous areas of life. Regardless of whether you're aware of it or not, Psychology is utilized in our regular day to day life, and with the correct tools, you also can use it to improve your experience by making simple improvements.

For what reason do you do the things you do? Regardless of our best endeavors to "know thyself," in all actuality, you frequently know minimal about our personalities, and even less about how others think. As Charles Dickens once put it, "A magnificent reality to consider, that each human animal is comprised to be that significant mystery and riddle to each other."

Therapists have long looked for bits of knowledge into how you see the world and what motivates our conduct, and they've made enormous strides in lifting that cover of the riddle. Besides giving fodder to mixed drink party discussions, the absolute most acclaimed psychological analyses of the previous century uncover widespread and regularly surprising realities about human instinct.

Here are ten exemplary psychological investigations that may change how you get yourself.

## *We as a whole have some limitations concerning evil*

Seemingly the most renowned analysis ever of, the 1971 Stanford jail study put a magnifying instrument on how social circumstances can influence human conduct. The scientists, driven by analyst Philip Zimbardo, set up a mock jail in the basement of the Stanford psych building and chose 24 students (who had no illicit record and were esteemed mentally healthy) to go about as detainees and gatekeepers. Specialists watched the detainees (who needed to remain in the cells 24 hours per day) and gatekeepers (who shared eight-hour shifts) utilizing concealed cameras.

The trial, which was booked to keep going for about fourteen days, must be stopped after only six days because of the gatekeepers' injurious conduct - sometimes they even perpetrated psychological torment - and the extraordinary emotional pressure and tension displayed by the detainees.

"The gatekeepers heightened their animosity against the detainees, stripping them exposed, and putting sacks over their heads, and afterward at long last had them participate in progressively mortifying sexual exercises," Zimbardo revealed to American Scientist. "Following six days, you needed to end it since it was crazy - you couldn't generally rest

72

during the evening without stressing what the watchmen could do to the detainees."

## We don't see what's right before us.

Think you know what's happening around you? You probably won't be as aware as you might suspect. In 1998, analysts from Harvard and Kent State University focused on walkers on school ground to decide how much individuals notice about their quick surroundings. In the trial, an entertainer came up to a person on foot and requested directions. While the person on foot was giving the instructions, two men conveying an enormous wooden entryway strolled between the entertainer and the passerby, totally hindering their perspective on one another for a few seconds. During that time, the actor was supplanted by another entertainer, one of alternate tallness, and with an alternative outfit, hairstyle, and voice. A full 50% of the members didn't see the substitution.

The investigation was one of the first to delineate the phenomenon of "change blindness," which shows precisely how specific you are about what you take in from some random visual scene - and it appears that you depend on memory and pattern-acknowledgment essentially more than you may suspect.

Postponing satisfaction is hard - however, we're increasingly successful when you do.

An acclaimed Stanford experiment from the late 1960s tried preschool youngsters' capacity to oppose the draw of instant satisfaction - and it yielded some powerful bits of knowledge about determination and self-restraint. In the test, four-year-olds were placed in a room without anyone else with a marshmallow on a plate before them and told that they could either eat the treat now or in the event that they held up until

73

the specialist returned 15 minutes after, they could have two marshmallows.

While the vast majority of the kids said they'd wait, they frequently attempted to oppose and afterward yielded, eating the treat before the scientist returned, TIME reports. The kids who managed to hold off for the full 15 minutes, for the most part, utilized avoidance strategies, such as turning away or covering their eyes. The ramifications of the youngsters' conduct were significant: Those who had the option to postpone delight were considerably less liable to be corpulent, or to have a chronic drug addiction or social issues when they were adolescents, and were increasingly successful later in life.

## *We can encounter profoundly conflicting moral motivations*

A renowned 1961 examination by Yale clinician Stanley Milgram tried (rather alarmingly) how far individuals would go to obey authority figures when requested to hurt others and the extreme inward clash between personal ethics and the commitment to obey specialist figures. Milgram needed to lead the investigation to give understanding into how Nazi war crooks could have propagated unspeakable acts during the Holocaust. To do as such, he tried a couple of members, one esteemed the "instructor" and the other considered the "student." The educator was told to direct electric stuns to the student (who was probably sitting in another room, however in all actuality was not being shocked) each time they got inquiries wrong. Milgram rather played recordings which made it sound like the student was in agony, and if the "educator" subject expressed a longing to stop, the experimenter pushed him to go on. During the experiment, 65 percent of members regulated a difficult, last 450-volt stun (marked "XXX"), albeit many were visibly focused and awkward about doing as such.

While the investigation has usually been viewed as a notice of visually impaired submission to authority, Scientific American as of late returned to it, contending that the outcomes were increasingly suggestive of profound moral conflict.

"Human good nature incorporates an affinity to be compassionate, kind and great to our fellow kin and group members, in addition to a tendency to be xenophobic, barbarous and shrewdness to innate others," writer Michael Shermer composed. "The stun analyses uncover not visually impaired submission but rather clashing moral propensities that lie deep inside."

As of late, some analysts have raised doubt about Milgram's philosophy, and one critic noticed that records of the analysis performed at Yale recommended that 60 percent of members really defied requests to regulate the most dosage shock.

### We're effectively debased by power.

There's a mental purpose for the way that people with significant influence some of the time demonstrate towards others with a feeling of entitlement and lack of respect. A recent report distributed in the diary Psychological Review placed students into groups of three to compose a short paper together. Two students were told to compose the paper, while the other was advised to assess the paper and decide how much every student would be paid. Amidst their work, an analyst got a plate of five treats. Albeit by and large the last treat was never eaten, the "manager" quite often ate the fourth treat - and ate it carelessly, mouth open.

"At the point when specialists give individuals control in logical examinations, they are bound to physically contact others in possibly wrong ways, to be a tease in more straightforward design, to settle on hazardous decisions and bets, to make first ideas in arrangements, to talk their brain, and to eat treats like the Cookie Monster, with morsels all over their jaws and chests," analyst Dacher Keltner, one of the investigation's chiefs, wrote in an article for UC Berkeley's Greater Good Science Center.

*We search out devotion to social groups and are effectively attracted to intergroup struggles.*

This great 1950s social psychology assessment sparkled a light on the conceivable mental premise of why social gatherings and nations end up entangled in strife with each other - and how they can figure out how to learn cooperation.

Study pioneer Muzafer Sherif took two gatherings of 11 young men (all age 11) to Robbers Cave State Park in Oklahoma for "day camp." The gatherings (named the "Hawks" and the "Rattlers") went through seven days separated, having a ton of fun together and bonding, with no learning of the presence of the other gathering. At the point when the two gatherings at last coordinated, the young men began calling each other names, and when they began contending in different recreations, more clash resulted and inevitably the gatherings would not eat together. In the following period of the examination, Sherif structured trials to attempt to accommodate the young men by having them enjoy recreation exercises together (which was ineffective) and afterward having them tackle an issue together, which at last started to facilitate the contention.

*We just need one thing to be glad.*

The 75-year Harvard Grant contemplate - a standout amongst the most extensive longitudinal investigations at any point directed - pursued 268 male Harvard students from the classes of 1938-1940 (presently very much into their 90s) for a long time, routinely gathering information on different parts of their lives. The all-inclusive end? Love truly is the only thing that is important, in any event with regards to deciding long joy and life fulfillment.

The examination's long-lasting chief, specialist George Vaillant, told The Huffington Post that there are two mainstays of joy: "One is love. The other is finding a method for adapting to a life that does not push love away." For instance, one member started the investigation with the most reduced rating for the future stability of the considerable number of subjects and he had previously endeavored suicide. So at the end of his life, he was one of the most joyful. Why? As Vaillant clarifies, "He went through his time on earth scanning for adoration."

***We flourish when we have solid confidence and societal position.***
Achieving distinction and progress isn't only a sense of self lift - it could likewise be a key to life span, as per the famous Oscar champs think about. Analysts from Toronto's Sunnybrook and Women's College Health Sciences Center found that Academy Award-winning on-screen characters and directors will, in general, live longer than the individuals who were nominated however lost, with winning entertainers and on-screen characters outlasting their losing peers by about four years.

"We are not saying that you will live more on the off chance that you win an Academy Award," Donald Redelmeier, the lead creator of the investigation, revealed to ABC News. "Or then again that individuals ought to go out and take acting courses. Our principle decision is just that social components are significant ... It recommends that an interior feeling of confidence is a significant angle to wellbeing and health services."

**We continually attempt to legitimize our encounters with the goal that they sound good to us.**

Any individual who's taken a first-year recruit Psych 101 class knows about intellectual disharmony, a hypothesis which manages that people have a characteristic habit to stay away from psychological conflict dependent on disharmonious or fundamentally unrelated convictions. In a regularly referred to 1959 analysis, therapist Leon Festinger solicited members to play out a sequence of dull assignments, such as turning pegs in a wooden handle, for 60 minutes. They were then paid either $1 or $20 to tell a "waiting individual" (otherwise known as a specialist) that the task was exceptionally intriguing. The individuals who were paid $1 to lie evaluated the assignments as more charming than the individuals who were paid $20. Their decision? The individuals who were paid more felt that they had adequate avocation for having played out the repetition task for 60 minutes, yet the individuals who were just paid $1 wanted to legitimize the time spent (and lessen the degree of discord between their convictions and their conduct) by saying that the activity was entertaining. As it were, you generally reveal to ourselves lies to show the world an increasingly sensible, amicable place.

**We buy into stereotypes in a big way.**

Stereotyping different gatherings of individual's dependent on the social group, ethnicity or class is something almost you all do, regardless of whether you try not to - and it can lead us to draw out of line and conceivably to harm decisions about the whole populace. NYU analyst John Bargh's investigations on "automaticity of social conduct" uncovered that you regularly judge individual's dependent on oblivious generalizations - and you can't resist the urge to follow up on them. You additionally will, in general, may get tied up with generalizations for

78

social gatherings that you see yourselves being a piece of. In one examination, Bargh found that a group of members who were approached to unscramble words identified with seniority - "Florida," "powerless" and "wrinkled" - strolled substantially slows down the foyer after the analysis than the gathering who unscrambled words random to age. Bargh rehashed the discoveries in two other practically identical examinations that authorized generalizations dependent on race and respectfulness.

"Stereotypes are classes that have gone excessively far," Bargh revealed to Psychology Today. "When you use generalizations, you take in the sex, the age, the color of the skin of the individual before us, and our brains react with messages that state unfriendly, dumb, moderate, and feeble. Those characteristics aren't out there in the environment. They don't reflect reality."

# Chapter 8

---

## *The 6 principles of persuasion*

Persuasion is a strategy that you use every day, except how influential would you say you are? When you are endeavoring to influence others, are you getting what you are looking for? If not, the time has come to begin working with your capacity to convince others. It is frequently felt that persuasion, and the systems that fall under it, is utilized for simple reasons, yet this isn't valid. Being great at belief makes a person to excel at work, in collaborating with outsiders and forming friendships.

A skill that you can develop with the right information and tips is persuasion. You can improve your persuasion aptitude by reading this book. This book explains the fundamentals of the belief that enables you to survey how successful you are right now. In this way, you can get a few noteworthy hints to improve your capacity to influence others.

For over sixty years, investigators have been studying various elements that impact you to say "yes" to the requests of others. There can be no uncertainty that there is a reason to how you are influenced, and a lot of the reasons that are behind it are surprising.

Whenever people are making a decision, they consider all the available information to guide their reasoning. However, the reality is different. As our lives are hectic and challenging, so to remove the burden, you often find other guidelines or routes to make decisions.

The six shortcuts that guide human conduct universally are recognized in research; they are:

- Scarcity
- Consistency
- Reciprocity
- Liking
- Consensus
- Authority

If you correctly understand these shortcuts and you apply them in a principled manner, then somehow anyone can be influenced by your request. Let's have a closer look at each alternative.

### The first principle of persuasion; reciprocity:

Mostly, people are grateful to give back the gift, behavior, or service that others have given them. For instance, if a friend invites you to his/her birthday party, it is necessary that you ask them to a party that you might be having in the future. If a coworker does you a service, then you are obligated to return that favor. People are more likely to say yes to those who have been grateful to them in the past.

The best demos to show the principle of reciprocity comes from a sequence of experiments conducted in restaurants. That means when you visited a restaurant at some point in past, the waiter or waitress might have given you a gift at the same time when they bring you the bill of your meal, this gift can be a cookie, a liqueur or a pure mint.

So the question is that the giving of a mint by the waitress or waiter to you as a gift, did it influence you on how much tip you are going to leave to them? Most people say no to this question. However, in recent studies, when people were given mint at the end of their meals, tips of the waiters or waitresses increased by three percent.

Amusingly, if the mint gift becomes doubled which means if two mints are given instead of two, the number of tips don't increase by two times but by four times that means a fourteen percent increase in tips.

Sometimes, when a waiter gives the person one mint, moves from the table, after a while turns his back and says, "this is an extra mint for such nice people" then there is a massive increase in the number of tips. The number of tips increases by about twenty-three percent. This is not because two mints were given, but it is about the way they were given. To use the reciprocity principle properly, you have to give first and what you give should be unexpected and modified.

### *The second principle of persuasion; scarcity*

Naturally, people need more of the things that they cannot have. For example, in 2003 when British Airways announced that the London-New York flight that flew twice in a day would no longer be operating because it was uneconomical to run, the next day sales took off.

Nothing changed about the flight. Its service didn't get better suddenly, it didn't fly faster, and the airfare didn't drop. It was just rarely available as a result people wanted more of it.

Hence, the reasons are transparent when it comes to using the scarcity principle for persuading others. To tell about the benefits the customers will acquire using your products is not enough. For your product to be well- known by people you need to point out what is unique in your product, how is it different from others and what will happen if people don't buy it i.e., tell about the losses that people can face not accepting your product.

### The third principle of persuasion; authority.

This principle is about the people that follow their leaders or experts having vast knowledge. For instance, physiotherapists can persuade a large number of patients to obey their recommended programs of exercise just by having their medical diplomas on the walls of their offices. People are not likely to give a change to a stranger wearing a uniform rather than casual clothes than to a parking meter.

Hence, what the science is teaching yourself is that first, it's essential that you prove yourself to people that you are knowledgeable and reliable rather than you start influencing them. This is a problematic situation; you cannot go around people telling them how much capable you are instead you can hire someone to do it for you. Shockingly, science tells you that the person who introduces you to people should not be only connected to you, but he is also succeeding from the introduction himself.

A group of real estate agents arranged staff who answered customer inquiries and told them about the expertise of the agents. In this way, the group of agents was able to increase the number of contracts and property appraisals.

Therefore, a staff member replied to the customers that were involved in letting a property as "Lettings? Let me connect you with Sandra; she has an experience of fifteen years in letting properties in the area". Similarly, customers who needed more information about selling properties were told by the staff member as "I will connect you to the head of sales department, Peter who has an experience of twenty years in selling properties."

The effect of this strategy led to an increase in the number of signed contracts by fifteen percent and an increase in the number of appointments by twenty percent. This was a considerable improvement despite being a small change, from persuasion science that was both priceless and moral to implement.

### *The fourth principle of persuasion is; consistency.*

Typically, people like to be constant with the things they have done previously or said. This principle activates when people are asking for or looking for small commitments to be made. For example, one set of studies shows that when researchers asked people to have wooden boards in their lawns at the front for the campaign of Drive safely, they were seen consistently refusing to the request.

Nevertheless, in a parallel area nearby, many house owners showed a willingness to four times as many homeowners indicated that they would be willing to put up the wooden board. This is because they decided to have a small postcard at the front side of their windows ten days previously to show support to the campaign of Drive Safely. This miniature postcard was the first commitment that little card was the initial commitment that led to a significant yet consistent change.

Thus, if a person of influence wants to persuade people by using the principle of consistency, he looks for active, voluntary, and public commitments. For instance, at a health center, the number of missed appointments were reduced by eighteen percent when the patients were asked to write the details of meeting in the future appointment card instead of the staff members writing for the patient.

### The fifth principle of persuasion; liking.

Generally, people say yes to those that they like.

But then how one person likes another? The science of persuasion talks about three fundamental factors; one you want people who praise us, you like people who are similar to our personalities, and you love people that help you to achieve common goals.

As the people are having more and more online interactions day by day so it would be worth asking whether these factors in such situations are effective or not.

At two famous business schools, a series of negotiation studies were carried out between MBA students, some groups of people were told, "Get straight down to business. Time is money". About fifty-five percent of people in this group agreed.

However, a second group was told, "Exchange some personal information with each other before you start negotiating. Recognize any similarity you might be sharing with the other person." About ninety percent of people in this group were able to come to a conclusion that was both agreeable and successful and was valued eighteen percent to both parties.

Hence, to use the principle of liking, you need to first look for characters that you might be sharing with others and the real compliments you can give before you start with your business.

### The sixth principle of persuasion; the consensus

Especially when people are uncertain about them, they will look at the behaviors and actions of other people to determine their own.

You might have observed that the hotel staff place small cards in washrooms to persuade guests to reuse the linens and towels. They do this to attract the attention of the guest on how reusing can have positive effects on the environment. This scheme turned out to be active leading to an agreement of about thirty-five percent. However, can there be a more effective way?

Well, about seventy-five percent of the people who check into a hotel for four days or more than that, they reuse the linens and towels at any point during the day. Thus you should take a lesson from the consensus principle that whatever is written on cards is beneficial for us. So, if people do what is written on postcards, then the reuse of towels increase by twenty-six percent.

At present picture the next time you stay in a hotel you saw one of these postcards or signs. You picked up the card and read the following message: "About seventy- five percent of the people that have stayed in this room have reused this towel." What will be your thoughts about it? Most likely, you will think, "I expect that these are not the same towels used by numerous people" Then like most people, this sign will not affect your behavior.

Nonetheless, when words were changed on the sign, the message was more productive, and about thirty-three percent of people reused towels as compared to the previous scenario. The science of persuasion is telling you that you should not rely all the time just on our abilities, but you should look at what others are doing in similar situations in which you are.

Hence, these were the six fundamental principles of persuasion that provide small cost less yet effective changes that can cause considerable differences in your persuasion skills within an ethical way. Therefore, they are called as the secrets of persuasion science.

# Chapter 9

---

## *Influencing mind by manipulation:*

## *Do you get manipulated?*

Manipulation may sound like an evil term; however, you can use it in actual during your daily routine life. Even you with your good intentions can use it for changing other's behaviors. Psychiatrists use this phenomenon every day. Police use it as they respond to any sort of argument. In fact, sometimes, you probably don't know, but people may manipulate you too. If you know how you can manipulate others, not just you can enhance your own quality of life, but also learn to counter similar techniques while they are practiced on you.

Almost always, manipulation involves deception. Most of the manipulators are the cleverest and accomplished liars. They consider lying as a form of art. They never only deceive you regarding who they are but also deceive you regarding what they do and why they do it. Deception and manipulation go in parallel. Few disturbed characters go beyond the irreverence for truth. Actually, they disdain this truth because it comes in their passage. And due to having their passage is their chief agenda, they lie for accomplishing it. This is what all about covert-aggression.

## The "Disguise" of Civility

Manipulators always want others to think good about them. Thus, they put on the disguises as the social facades of the civility. However, underlying they are quite ruthless and connivers – they try to get the good of you while pretending to be good. Many times, you can easily see through their superficial and shallowness in time. However, sometimes, you fail to get to it. Also, it is not your fault always as you fail to see it. Few folks are good at this art of managing their impressions. You, eventually, may learn who they are in real and what they are all about in real. However, that's generally long after you get conned by them already. It is just like to get whiplash. You understand what has happened soon after they had caused you damage.

## Character and Honesty

It is not sufficient to only get willing to accept the truth. A lot of folks do this, particularly after getting caught lying. Instead, it is vital to revere that truth truly. If you have a solid character, you would know the worth of truth – it has the power of healing, of empowering and of freedom. However, you always have a choice of embracing the truth. This choice is made by all those fellows who have decent characters in actual. Most of the future manipulators become wrong in their character's development is an adverse relation they form with speaking truth. The determination they have, often they see the truth coming in their way. So, they get to learn only about how they can play fastest and loose with the play so that they acquire what they desire. With time, they may become strangers to the truth regarding themselves as well as the truth regarding their intentions. Meanwhile, they get to learn about pulling the curtain oversight of other people.

## Does everyone get manipulated?

How much damage occurs when you fall for the manipulators? – for few people, it can be like losing out on their jobs promotions, getting their pension taken into a bad investment, come to know quite late that some people you admire are hiding their double lives from you, or getting traumatized or murdered.

As you hear regarding the people that get callously destroyed, conned and hurt by their friends or when you hear the news which generally leaves questions in your mind like "could someone have stopped them?" or "how people get away with this?" The answer is that often they can be stopped if danger signs weren't overlooked. One of the ideal methods of catching manipulators before they wreak havoc on your lives is to use honing your behavioral analysis skills.

Many human beings can detect deception without any training, with around 50% of accuracy. Maneuvering and reading manipulations are the skills, and they can be enhanced upon. Whether you deal with a lover, a co-worker, a stranger or a friend, such skills are quite valuable. Far beyond ignoring your loss of pride which comes along with getting manipulated, you can avoid losing the money, the life, or the sanity on the potential basis if you become able to spot the manipulators in their act. There exist three sections for detecting manipulators: norming, noticing common non-verbal signs of deception and to spot the verbal signals.

## *Norming*

Nearly every human being has a usual method of being or a base-line. For norming anyone, you require of finding his/her baseline or the way he/she acts as he/she is at ease (the concept got the fame by a former agent of ATF and an expert of body language, Janine Driver). It is easy to read out people which you know well as you've had enough time for norming them and then learn the way they see as they are triggered or calm in any way. You perform it without having any thoughts, and it is one of the eldest survival mechanisms which human beings use. To be able to identify drastic and quick changes in the behavior of other people which warn you to impend violence or activate deception can be highly useful if you learn to stop ignoring your gut feeling. Similar to the polygraph tests, finding out the truth has a link with spotting differences in the demeanor of a person. Ro develops an accurate baseline of people can make it easy to find out when people are reacting and what sort of reaction they are showing.

When people norm anyone, they do quick scanning of their body gestures and pay particular attention to peculiar behaviors:

- **Feet** –Where are they directed? Do they cross each other? What is the width of their true stance? Know that feet present around 12 to 18 inches apart show a confident stance.
- **Hands**— are they clenched, or are they open? Do they carry any visible weapon? Are they concealing up any part of the body? Do they get engage by self-soothing (picking or rubbing other parts of the body for regulating intense emotions? Like, playing with rings or picking at a hangnail.
- **Torso**—do they point to or away from you? The belly button or torso direction is the best sign of who gets the full attention.
- **Head-** what kind of facial expressions do they make? Do have narrowed gaze with pursed lips ready to attack? Do they carry a real smile or a fake smile?
- **Voice Tone**– do they have high pitch normally? Do they try to be more confident in the moment? Do they get strained nervousness?
- **Verbal and Language Cues**– why another person seems unwilling to giving you a clear and straight reply? What is the purpose of everything they are saying?

To get in the habit of watching people at the public places can be quite a good method of building up the norming skills. Body gestures, speech tones, verbal sign, and even pupil dilation or blinking can play a vital role to norm anyone. Alcohol can intensify emotional expressions and reduce inhibitions. It can get easier to located an exaggerated expression of anger, to be territorial, completion, sadness, or seduction in the bars. Look for the norm of a person and after that, pay closer attention to when his/her attitude changes.

## *Common Signs for Deception or CCD*

Now that you get to know how you can norm others, it will get easier to imply this list of the common signs for deception for increasing your behavioral awareness. If you understand what to search for, it will get easy to locate these signs as they occur and not overlook your instinct feeling. If you notice anyone showing any of these signs, it may not mean necessarily that they are deceiving or that they are lying intentionally. But, these signs may show that they are uncomfortable, trying to win approval or simply nervous. It is totally up to you to choose how you can use this information.

Manipulators and practiced liars try to perform the opposite of what you have learned regarding lies. Thus, how can you spot these lies? Search for those who appear to be helpful or those who are uncomfortably friendly.

**CCD's:**

- For creating a false intimacy, violating the personal space – to lean in very close, to step into the personal bubble even after you step back for re-adjusting and touching your shoulder or arm repeatedly for trying to make a rapport.
- A deeper gaze or an increased contact through eyes
- Continuous mirroring of the body language (often, the salesperson is trained for doing this).
- False smile – muscles around eye contracts and make the smile lines like a real smile is being shown.

- A voice within you tells you that this seems wrong! - The unpracticed manipulators may face discomfort or fear around an act of manipulation or lying. The most common cues of this discomfort are self-touching, making a barrier using arm and averting gaze.
- Self-soothing or self-touching – playing with the hair, rubbing the neck, hugging oneself, playing with the jewelry, etc.
- Avoiding eye contact
- To bring hands and fingers up to mouth – this is a subconscious activity for blocking the comfortability thing to come out of the mouth.
- To rub the nose
- Stiff, unnatural and limited body movements

- Making barriers – coffee, books, and crossing of arms can be utilized for creating a barrier if a person becomes uncomfortable whilst a discussion. Many times, when people become uncomfortable regarding what they say, they also make a barrier in front of the mouth. This is the big reason why they don't believe in the use of a desk or a podium while they lecture, run workshops, or train. To keep an open stance to gain trust and build support is paramount.

If you observe any of these signs, it is the time to start keeping an eye onto the person that is exhibiting these signs.

## *Verbal Signs*

After that, you get an understanding about how you can norm, common non-verbal cues of deception and now is the time to bring in the whole deal together. Manipulators leave the cues for you. Even skilled ones do this. If you are vigilant and observant, you can spot a lot of verbal manipulators that leave behind in anyone's quest for powering over you. Few verbal indicators provide you an intent of manipulation. Can you identify these cues before?

- **A lot of details**- one of the most common technique is the over usage of the descriptors for trying to prove the realistic approach of the story.

- **Mumbling or changes in voice pitch** – intense use of emotions can turn your vocal cords into constrictions causing the high pitch voices. Manipulators or lairs understand that people having a deeper voice are regarded as trustworthy. To speak in the monotone voices or the sharp sounds can signal that you are nervous or tending to control you're your actual emotions or thoughts.

- **Loan sharking or the help which comes with a cost** – did someone offers you anything free of cost without asking anything in return; you would take it reluctantly, and after then, they ask something like a return, and it seems that it would be a big sacrifice form your side? People that need to acquire control over themselves may provide your assistance or help for building a rapport and then try to exploit the false link by praying over your sense of the reciprocal treatment.

94

- **Sociopathic bragging** – master manipulators or sociopaths take tremendous pride in their skills for gaining control and power over others. People often share their info which can save you easily from a lot of misery, if you keep your eyes open be staying at a distance from them. Pay close attention to sharing which people perform during job interviews, on dates. It can show quite a lot.

# Chapter 10

## *How to use deception to influence minds*

An act, whether big or small, cruel or kind that makes someone believe something untrue is called deception. The results of various studies showed that an average man lies several times a day, which means even honest people practice the act of fraud in their lives. It depends upon lies also such as big lies like "I have never cheated on you," then there are little white lies like "that dress looks fine." Such myths are set up to either dodge uncomfortable situations or spare someone's emotions Deception isn't always done to other people. Sometimes, some people lie to themselves from saying that they are confident to dangerous misconceptions that are not under their control. Although it is harmful to a person to lie to himself, however, some researchers argue that there are different types of self-deception, for instance, a person believing in accomplishing a goal that he cannot achieve.

Investigators have researched for a long time to find out ways whether a person is lying or not. One of the famous tests is the polygraph test. This test is still being considered controversial as it cannot show proper results when measuring psychiatric people having a disorder like Antisocial Personality disorder. Such mental disorders cannot be correctly measured by polygraphs or other lie- detection techniques.

## Why We Lie

No one likes being betrayed, and when famous people are caught in a lie, it results in a major scandal. Although some people have pride in their real personality and they try to distance themselves from people who deceive, actually such people also lie for various reasons. Surprisingly, scientists say that to maintain a healthy life, a certain amount of deception is excellent for society to function. The field of deception was studied by theologians and ethicists but now psychologists are also interested to know the reasons why people lie or the circumstances that make them do so.

## How to use deception with truthful words?

Business directors regularly use smart strategies to get a better deal during discussions—usually making statements that are theoretically true but are purposely twisted to deceive the other side.

Such form of deception is called paltering. The act of using truthful words to affect a targets belief although having a false or partial impression. However, it's not only the businessmen who palter but famous figures like Bill and Hilary Clinton even Donald Trump has done it too. Yet you might have paltered.

Some of the recent research shows that people who palter feel nothing wrong about it, but on the receiving end, people think they have been betrayed. People who palter may have beneficial deals for some time, but if they use paltering for a long time, their cunning ways can be recognized, which can ruin their relationship with other people. It was written in a newspaper once that "Deceitful Paltering: The Rewards and Dangers of Using Honest Speeches to Betray Others."

A co-author at the Harvard Business School as a Tandon Family, Professor of Business Administration, serving in the Negotiations, Organizations & Markets Unit once said: "it's interesting to see the change between the person who is betrayed and the person who betrayed him." "People think that using this method they are telling the truth and they are honest but, the people who are deceived think that they are as dishonest as if they lie straight to their face."

### The different forms of deception.

The fact is, lying is frequent.

Past investigations have shown that commonly, an average man lies once or twice a day to a family member, friends, partner, or co-workers. But most of them are little white lies that are harmful.

However, some lies are, which can result in stressful situations. Other myths are more severe and can lead to severe consequences. Deception can significantly change the outcomes of negotiations that are dependent on information.

Paltering is different from other practices of deception:

• The active use of incorrect statements from lying by commission, for instance, claiming the defective transmission on a vehicle works great.

• Another is lying by omission, which means holding back vital information—for example, not mentioning any information about the faulty transmission of a vehicle.

The investigators held six experiments and two pilot studies to examine the three different deceptive tactics used in various contexts involving online negotiations and face to face interactions.

In one experiment, they asked the participants to imagine a situation: your sales have grown consistently over the last ten years, but the next year you expect the sales to flat. If you are asked by your colleague "What do you expect about the sales next year?" the answer will be different depending on the kind of deceptive tactic used.

• If you answer using lie by the commission, then your answer would be: "I think the sales will grow next year." In such a situation, you are deceiving your co-worker by providing him incorrect information.

• If you respond by using lie by omission, you will remain silent when your colleague says, "I think sales will go up next year just like they have been in the past ten years." Thus, you are not correcting his false belief.

• If you use paltering, then you might say, "Well you know how our sales have grown consistently in the past ten years." This response is precisely accurate, but it doesn't focus on your anticipation that sales will be flat in the coming year, and you know that it is going to create a false impression by your colleague that sales will go up.

When the participants were told the definitions of lying by omission, paltering and lying by commission, the majority of them were able to categorize their answers correctly which means that they understood the meaning of these tactics.

### *Paltering is common.*

Skilled negotiators tell that they participate in paltering more often as they lie by omission then they lie by the commission.

Actually, in one of the pilot studies in HBS Executive Education course that enlisted business executives of number 184 mid- to senior-level, all of them as a part of their business activities in various industries negotiate. Fifty-two percent of them stated that they used paltering in some or most of their negotiations while about twenty-one percent of them stated that they used to lie by omission tactic.

Possibly they use paltering more because they don't feel bad about it compared to complete lying palter more often because it doesn't make them feel as bad as outright lying. The investigators have found that negotiators think that paltering is more morally tolerable than both lying by omission and lying by commission

People who use lie by the commission have trouble rationalizing their conduct in their minds because they know that they are giving false statements. Perhaps, many business directors think that there is nothing wrong in doing paltering. They focus on the accuracy of their comments, thus feel justified while doing paltering thinking like," I spoke the truth." In some instances, they blame the target by saying that he should have paid closer attention to what they were talking about instead considering that they had a misleading impression.

What is the reason that people use paltering? It's simple. Most of the business managers about eighty-eight percent of them accepted that using paltering they can have beneficial business deals.

Gino states, "People don't answer the questions they are asked when they palter." "In a lot of negotiations, there is a temptation to deceive, so you end up with a better deal, or at least this is what people tend to believe, especially in situations where they are claiming value."

The reason that paltering is common is that it works. Palters cannot be easily recognized. Thus, they usually get away by betraying others to gain a larger share of revenues.

### The risks of paltering.

Investigators found through various experiments that the risks concerned with paltering are huge and sometimes dangerous. If the deception is exposed, the negotiations will result in a deadlock, and by doing so, the negotiators can ruin their statuses that can eternally break their relations with people and other associations.

It is due to the reason that targets of paltering feel deceived, and that is why they consider this practice as immoral as lying commission is.

That's because targets of paltering feel fooled and consider the practice to be just as dishonest as lying by commission. Participants stated that due to deception, they were less likely to negotiate with people again. Gino states, "It's almost impossible for the negotiators to understand that the world is really small". "Most of the times, when you use deception in negotiations, people figure it out. In this case, the status is harmed to a level that you cannot negotiate with the same person again. You are so concentrated on the short term that you don't realize what you can face in the future because of using this tactic."

It is even a worse situation when a person is asked a question, and he chooses to palter compared to spontaneous paltering. An investigator's write says, "In few cases, deceiving targets in reply to a direct question is considered more immoral than deceiving targets actively."

Gino has seen directly the loss paltering can do during her negotiation exercises in her MBA classes.

She states, "In our class, we have some interesting discussions. People say to the person they choose to deceive: "I didn't lie to you." Indeed, they didn't lie, but they also gave a false impression. "And the people who are targeted consider them liars and keep their rage within them through the complete semester. The people who become targets of lies, develop extreme feelings that adversely affects the people around them, and it also affects their interaction with people."

Gino hopes that different research studies will provide a moral lesson to business directors or executives that they will understand: be careful of bending the truth during negotiations.

She states, "We are so concentrated on our side during negotiations."

"Negotiators need to understand that no matter they are stating the true statements, but the receiving side might see they're doing in a way that might damage their relationship in the future. People should be aware of the outcomes they can face due to various negotiating techniques."

## *What Are the Basic Rules People Exploit When Lying?*

To comprehend the vocal tactics, you use to betray each other – it helps to recognize how the general discussion works.

A famous researcher named Paul Grice noticed that people follow a basic set of rules when having conversations with one another.

Every time you talk to a person, you do follow the maxims (Grice's rules).

It would be impossible to have a conversation without following these rules. As everyone follows the rules, but the majority of them are not aware of them and their use. Grice's rules usually work in the background that you are not mindful of.

What could be the unspoken rules you follow when speaking to each other?

The four basic Grice's rules or maxims are:

## *Maxim of Quality*

As stated by the first rule – people are likely to say what they know to be valid. When speaking to one other – you anticipate that people will tell you the truth.

For instance, if your husband/wife asks, "...have you seen the keys of my vehicle?" An authentic answer is expected.

## *Maxim of Quantity*

When people are having a conversation, one must provide the necessary information to get to the point. People should not either give too little information nor too much information.

Therefore, when your partner asks after you get to home from an important meeting, "What happened today?" you should respond to the question neither with too little information such "Nothing much" nor too much information such as "I sat by the door, the meeting started five minutes late, etc."

## *Maxim of Relation*

As stated by this rule, you should remain connected to the topic being discussed. Mainly, you should make statements relevant to the topic being discussed. You should not add irrelevant information.

If your partner asks, "How was your day?" and you respond by saying, "I detest tomatoes" then you are not following the principles, you are relied upon to make a statement that is to some degree should be related to the current topic.

## Maxim of Manner

To end with, the last rule states that your remarks should be direct, to the point and clear. You should not use ambiguous and vague language when making comments.

If your boyfriend asks, "How does my new shirt look" and you react by saying, "it's intriguing", you are not following the Maxim of Manner, you need to direct and clear.

Generally, these simple rules of conversation are beneficial – both when they are followed and when they are not followed.

## Following the Rules/Maxims

When people follow the conversational rules, it is easy to understand each other. Whatever they say is direct, explicit, and to the point.

## Noticeably Breaking the Rules/Maxims

These rules, when broken, are still useful in some way. For instance, if a person violates the easily noticeable laws, you try to think about why this happened. "Why did she say that."

The following illustrations express how this works:

If somebody asks you, "What amount did your home expense?" and you react by saying that "Enough," well, ideally they will get the point, "it's not your issue to worry about."

This is how it is suggested meaning; you must express things without really saying them by disrupting Grice's guidelines.

One more case of violating the rules/maxims: imagine that you and a companion at work are lounging around work grumbling about your supervisor. Mid-sentence, your companion, unexpectedly switches the point, thus breaking the rule of relation. Without saying a word, your companion has told what you have to know.

When you want to be unambiguously direct and clear, you follow the critical Grice's rules

Also, you disrupt the norms in an obvious, observable way to cause a point without having to be unequivocal about the point being made. You also may misuse these rules when you are trying to betray one another.

### How Not to Get Duped

Pride, as most feelings, is a piece of human instinct. But since its frequently treated as a positive characteristic, it opens you to being tricked, first by ourselves, trailed by other individuals.

### Thus how can we battle these propensities as leaders?

Concede, you may not be right. In his renowned collection of memoirs, Benjamin Franklin composes of his choice to begin conceding that he could not be right when he put forward contentions. He said that by doing that, and by listening to individuals when he couldn't help contradicting with them as opposed to bouncing in with his very own perspective, he decreased his dread of being wrong.

Make it a standard to avoid every single direct logical inconsistency to the opinions of others, and all positive affirmation of my own. You can even have precluded me from the utilization of each word or articulation in the language that imported a fixed assessment, for example, "positively," "without a doubt," and so forth. You have adopted rather than the "I apprehend" "I consider" or "I envision" or so "it appears to me at present."

At the point when another attested something that you thought a mistake, you prevented me from the delight of negating him suddenly, and of demonstrating him some irrationality in his suggestion. When in answering, you may have started by seeing that in specific cases or conditions, his assessment would be correct, however in the present fact there showed up or seemed to be some distinction, and so on. You will have soon found out the benefit of this change in my behavior: the discussions you were occupied with went on more satisfyingly. The unobtrusive manner by which you proposed my conclusions secured them a readier reception and less logical inconsistency. You have had less embarrassment when you were observing yourself to be in the wrong state, and you'll have the more effectively won with others to surrender their errors and unite with yourself when you have happened to be morally justified.

This technique fundamentally made Franklin less prideful. Given Konnikova's exploration, it is sensible to expect that he was tricked less by himself and others as a result of it.

Be happy to alter your perspective totally. Your inspirations must be to keep up decent notoriety opens us up to being cheated. Composes Konnikova, "Even after, in spite of our earnest attempts at self-daydream, it ends up evident that you have been shown a good time.... our reputational inspiration will be sufficiently able to keep us calm".

Pioneers who are eager to change positions in light of new information irrespective of social results are more reluctant to fall into the pride trap. In a fast company article, a year ago, you expounded on how Elon Musk has an exceptional blend of headship attributes: stubborn enough to move individuals, yet versatile enough to be inventive. Musk doesn't appear to fear to look awful if he is off-base about something. He frames such blunders in terms of data accessibility: if he is wrong about something. It was due to the reason that his comprehension of the world has changed totally, and that is impeccably right.

106

As the Arbinger Institute expresses, "self-duplicity" …. blinds you to the genuine reasons of issues, and once you are visually impaired, every one of the "solutions" you can consider will exacerbate the situation." There might be momentary political implications to conceding your blunders, yet the activity of a kind pioneer is to influence individuals to make the best choice.

To do that, you must need self-confidence, not to fall for it.

## Simple Test for Deception

Individuals frequently claim that they are not deceiving others even though they are deliberately withholding important data from them. Individuals prefer to think as such because that makes it simpler for them to betray others.

Thus, a good test checks whether you are deceiving somebody is as following:

• If you don't have anything to hide, why not tell the whole truth? This is generally the ideal approach to decide whether you are deluding somebody, irrespective of your intent.

As you can see this meaning of deception is exceptionally expansive: it includes a broad scope of behaviors. However, there is a valid reason for seeing deception this way.

When pondering our very own misleading conduct, you like to think in exceptionally restricted and specialized terms – like telling somebody an explicit misrepresentation. It is to our most significant advantage to think like this; it makes you feel both less remorseful and less responsible for your conduct.

Taking such a narrow perspective on deception causes you to keep up a positive self-image, which makes it simpler to misdirect others. It is simpler to swindle somebody when you don't think about your conduct as being misleading.

This is significant, given that most deception happens through methods other than lying. Indeed, deception is regularly best achieved by what is left implied (clarified in detail on the page that pursues).

However, then again, when you find that a friend or family member has been acting in a manner which leads you to believe in things that are not valid, our meaning of duplicity abruptly turns out to be increasingly comprehensive (expansive).

With regards to deception, individuals will, in general, be a somewhat enormous hypocrite. When you forget significant subtleties, I'm not deceiving you, yet when you do likewise to me, it feels beguiling.

Think about the example of Brad and Spencer for a moment. In what manner may Spencer respond, if she somehow happened to find that Brad and Denise really like one another and they might be flirting behind her back? Do you think Spencer will be any more joyful realizing that Brad (and Denise) didn't tell a single lie?

This is the reason a full meaning of deception is more helpful than a narrow perspective. The deep sense of deception is just progressively legit.

# Conclusion

Dark Psychology is the investigation of the human condition as it relates with the rational nature of individuals to go after other people persuaded by deviant or criminal drives that lack reasons and general presumptions of instinctual drives and sociology hypothesis. All of humankind can deceive different people and living animals. While many control or sublimate this inclination, some follow up these motivations. Dark psychology looks to comprehend those feelings, perceptions, thoughts, and abstract preparing systems that lead to ruthless conduct that is contradictory to contemporary understandings of human behavior. Dark psychology expects that deviant, criminal, and harsh practices are purposive and have some goal or objective behind it ninety-nine percent of the time. It proposes there is a district inside the human's brain that empowers a few people to carry out appalling acts without reason. Dark psychology is a standout amongst the most dominant powers at work on the planet today. The most dominant influencers utilize it. It is utilized by the most foremost influencers the world has ever known. The individuals who are uninformed of it risk having it used against them. Try not to run that risk!

All ordinary people have feelings, thoughts, and perceptions, but some people impulsively use them while others learn how to control them. Psychology, philosophy, religion, and other different creeds have tried cogently to define dark psychology. It is a fact, most human behavior that is related to evil actions is objective and purposive oriented, yet dark psychology presumes that there is a zone where objective oriented inspiration and purposive conduct appear to be vague. Hence, you might not know these people are around you. It depends upon the condition of the individual, whether it's normal or worse. Dark psychology talks about dark traits.

Both world history and regular daily existence are brimming with instances of individuals acting heartlessly, selfishly or vindictively. In both common language and psychology, such dark propensities of human are named narcissism (unreasonable self-retention), psychopathy (absence of compassion), and Machiavellianism (the conviction that standard rules don't apply in any situation), the alleged dark triad of three, alongside numerous others, for example, sadism, egoism or spitefulness.

Typically, not everyone has such dark characteristics; it depends upon your psyche and how you behave with people. That is why specialists such as psychologists study the behavior of people to know the reasons why a specific person possesses such characters. Want to know about dark psychology? This book explains some of the essential principles of dark psychology. Every chapter of this book clarifies a part of dark psychology that can be easily understood by a common man with no specialist knowledge. By studying different examples and cases, your concept of dark psychology will become crystal clear. Reading this book, you will be able to understand the psyche of people who use black magic and the reasons behind their dangerous motives. Thus, you should read this book and get to know about the world of black magic.

CPSIA information can be obtained
at www.ICGtesting.com
Printed in the USA
LVHW080128300621
691543LV00004B/391